Writing Engagement
Involving Students in the
Writing Process:
Grade 8

By
JANET P. SITTER, Ph.D.

COPYRIGHT © 2002 Mark Twain Media, Inc.

ISBN 1-58037-207-4

Printing No. CD-1553

Mark Twain Media, Inc., Publishers
Distributed by Carson-Dellosa Publishing Company, Inc.

Table of Contents

Table of Contents

Introduction

This book is a writing engagement resource for both teachers and students. Through these exercises, students will improve both their writing and their language skills. By evaluating their writing using the rubrics in the book, students will sharpen their understanding of the writing process and their writing skills. Teachers will have a consistent process for teaching and evaluating student writing using the assessment rubrics provided.

There are five important features emphasized in this book: (1) the practice and apply student work pages; (2) the teacher evaluation rubrics; (3) the student writing rubrics; (4) the student writing prompts; and (5) the writing skills tests.

The Writing Process

1. **Prewriting:** Choose a topic; gather and organize ideas; identify the audience for the writing; identify the purpose of the writing; choose the appropriate format for the writing.

2. **Drafting:** Write a rough draft to get down the ideas; write beginnings that "grab" the reader's attention; emphasize ideas rather than mechanics.

3. **Revising:** Share writing with the group or teacher; reflect on comments and make substantive changes; prepare a clean draft.

4. **Editing:** Proofread narratives carefully; help others proofread; identify and correct mechanical errors.

5. **Publishing:** Publish writing in an appropriate form; share writing with an appropriate audience.

Section I: Writing for a Purpose and an Audience

Purpose: Am I writing to entertain? To inform? To persuade? To describe?

Audience: Am I writing for myself to express and clarify my ideas and/or feelings? Or am I writing for others? Possible audiences include my peers, younger children, parents, grandparents, children's authors, pen pals, etc.

Unit 1: Writing to Express Ideas

Purpose: Writing to learn and explore ideas and problems

Audience: Usually done for general, unknown audiences

Unit 2: Writing to Influence

Purpose: Writing to convince someone or sway his or her opinion to accept the writer's way of thinking

Audience: The audience may be known or unknown.

Unit 3: Writing to Inform

Purpose: Writing to share information with others

Audience: The audience may be known or unknown.

Unit 4: Writing to Entertain or Create

Purpose: Writing to create fictitious stories, true stories, poetry, or plays to entertain others

Audience: The audience may be classmates, family, or other trusted audiences.

Unit 1: Everyday Writing

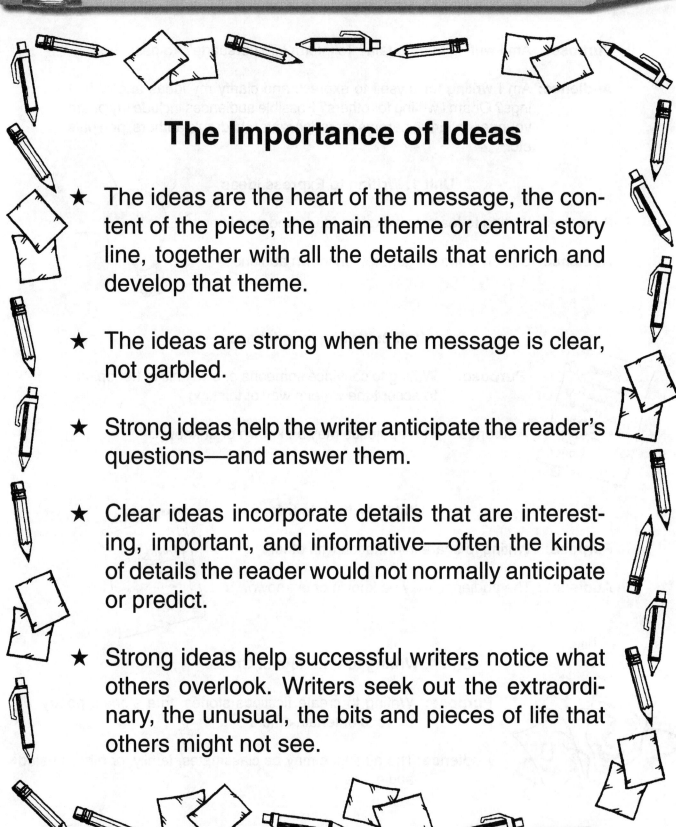

The Importance of Ideas

★ The ideas are the heart of the message, the content of the piece, the main theme or central story line, together with all the details that enrich and develop that theme.

★ The ideas are strong when the message is clear, not garbled.

★ Strong ideas help the writer anticipate the reader's questions—and answer them.

★ Clear ideas incorporate details that are interesting, important, and informative—often the kinds of details the reader would not normally anticipate or predict.

★ Strong ideas help successful writers notice what others overlook. Writers seek out the extraordinary, the unusual, the bits and pieces of life that others might not see.

Name: _____ Date: _____

Topic: _____

Type of Writing: _____

1. Scoring Rubric for Evaluating Ideas

Directions: Circle the number that best describes the quality of the writing.

1 **Not Yet:**   A bare beginning; writer not yet showing any control
2 **Emerging:**   Need for revision outweighs strengths; isolated moments hint at what the writer has in mind
3 **Developing:** Strengths and need for revision are about equal; about halfway home
4 **Effective:**   On balance, the strengths outweigh the weaknesses; a small amount of revision is needed
5 **Strong:**   Shows control and skill in this trait; many strengths present
6 **Wow!**   Exceeds expectations

Features	Not Yet	Emerging	Developing	Effective	Strong
Ideas:	**1**	**2**	**3**	**4**	**5**
	This paper has no clear sense of purpose or central theme. To extract meaning from the text, the reader must make inferences based on sketchy or missing details. The writing reflects more than one of these problems. *The writer is still in search of a topic, brainstorming, or has not yet decided what the main idea of the piece will be. *Information is limited or unclear, or the length is not adequate for development. *The idea is a simple restatement of the topic or an answer to the question with little or no attention to detail. *The writer has not begun to define the topic in a meaningful, personal way. *Everything seems as important as everything else; the reader has a hard time sifting out what is important. *The text may be repetitious, or it may read like a collection of disconnected, random thoughts with no discernible point.	This writer is beginning to define the topic, even though development is still basic or general. *The topic is fairly broad; however, you can see where the writer is headed. *Support is attempted, but doesn't go far enough yet in fleshing out the key issues or story line. *Ideas are reasonably clear, though they may not be detailed, personalized, accurate, or expanded enough to show in-depth understanding or a strong sense of purpose. *The writer seems to be drawing on knowledge or experience but has difficulty going from general observations to specifics. *The reader is left with questions. More information is needed to fill in the blanks. *The writer generally stays on the topic but does not develop a clear theme. The writer has not yet focused the topic past the obvious.		This paper is clear and focused. It holds the reader's attention. Relevant anecdotes and details enrich the central theme. *The topic is narrow and manageable. *Relevant, telling, quality details give the reader important information that goes beyond the obvious or predictable. *Reasonably accurate details are present to support the main ideas. *The writer seems to be writing from knowledge or experience; the ideas are fresh and original. *The reader's questions are anticipated and answered. *Insight—an understanding of life and a knack for picking out what is significant—is the indicator of high-level performance, though not required.

Comments: _____

_____

Name: _____ Date: _____

Unit 1: Student Writing Rubric—Ideas

Topic: _____

Type of Writing: *Expository*   *Persuasive*   *Narrative*

Directions: Check those statements that apply to your piece of writing.

_____   I have a clear and interesting topic.

_____   My writing is based on my own experience or my own investigation of the topic.

_____   I can sum up my main point in one sentence:

_____

_____

_____   My beginning "grabs" my readers' attention and makes them want to read more.

_____   All my sentences are important to the topic.

_____   I included all important events in the order of their happening.

_____   I *show* things happening rather than *telling* about them.

_____   I have a strong ending that leaves my readers satisfied.

_____   My readers aren't left with any important unanswered questions.

Comments: _____

_____

_____

_____

_____

_____

_____

Name: _____ Date: _____

Unit 1: Writing a Personal Journal

Key Ideas

- **Journal writing** is a way of recording your private thoughts and ideas.

- **Journals** can be private (like a diary) or can be shared with others (like a personal narrative).

Practice

Directions: Read the journal prompt, and then write your response on the lines below. Share your entry with others if you wish.

> Write about the most memorable person you have ever known.
> Who is it? What makes him or her memorable?

_____

_____

_____

_____

_____

_____

_____

_____

_____

_____

_____

_____

On Your Own: Begin to keep a journal, if you don't already. Find the kind of notebook you like to write in and the kind of pen or pencil you prefer to use, and write a daily entry about your thoughts, feelings, ideas, etc.

Name: _____ Date: _____

Unit 1: Writing a Journal

Key Ideas

- **Journal writing** is a way of recording your private thoughts and ideas.

- **Journals** can be private (like a diary) or can be shared with others (like a personal narrative).

- The best **journals** are rich in detail and record what the writer saw, heard, thought, felt, did, and so on.

Practice

Directions: Choose one of the three journal prompts and write about it on the lines below.

1. Are you a nobody or a somebody? Which would you rather be?
2. If I could change something about myself, I'd change ...
3. Choose a color that best describes you and explain why.

_____

_____

_____

_____

_____

_____

_____

_____

_____

_____

_____

_____

_____

On Your Own: Using a special notebook and writing tool, keep a daily journal of your thoughts and opinions. Keep your writing private.

Name: _____ Date: _____

Unit 1: Writing a Dialogue Journal

Key Ideas

- A **dialogue journal** contains an exchange of writing between a student and a teacher.

- A **dialogue journal** is a good way to clear up confusion or to ask a question not asked in class.

Practice:

Directions: Read the dialogue journal between Jon and his teacher.

Dear Mrs. Taylor,

    I am really learning a lot in science class and like this unit that we are doing. However, I am confused about what you said today. I didn't want to ask during class because I didn't want to be embarrassed.

    Here is my question: How can a laser beam be used to cut something? Is this possible?

    I hope you can answer my question.

Thanks,
Jon

Dear Jon,

    Laser beams are quickly replacing knives as cutting tools. They are so precise they are often replacing scalpels in surgery. When the heat from the laser is intense enough to cut, it also seals the wound around the cut, thus doing double duty.

    Keep asking questions, Jon!

Mrs. T.

Now you try writing a dialogue journal. On your own paper, draw a line down the page vertically. Think of something that you have learned in class, something you may be confused about, or something you may have a question about. Perhaps you want to ask your teacher something but haven't felt able to do this yet. A dialogue journal would be a good place to start. When you have edited your writing for ideas and content, hand it in for your teacher's response.

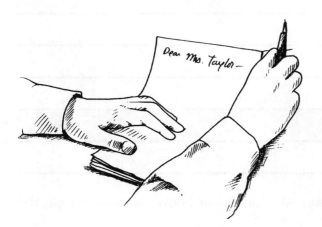

On Your Own: Start a dialogue journal with one of your teachers or with another student. Try to write on a regular basis. If you choose a teacher, be patient. Teachers are very busy, and it may take a while for your teacher to respond. (This usually isn't a problem if you pick another student.)

Name: _____ Date: _____

Unit 1: Writing a Business Letter

Key Ideas

- The **business letter** has a standard format that must be followed if the writer wants to make a good impression and accomplish his/her purpose.

- A **business letter** format contains the:
  - **Heading** – includes the address of the person sending the letter and the date it was written.
  - **Inside address** – includes the full address of the person or firm to whom the letter is being sent.
  - **Salutation** – the greeting can be in one of two forms. If the name of the recipient is known, use that name; for example, *Dear Mr. Brown:*. If the name of the recipient is unknown, use *Gentlemen:, Dear Sir:,* or *Dear Madam:*.
  - **Body** – the part of the letter where the business takes place. It should be short, concise, clear, and polite.
  - **Closing** – consists of any polite closing: *Respectfully, Sincerely, Cordially, Very truly yours,* etc.
  - **Signature** – the name of the sender is typed three lines below the closing, and the signature is handwritten between the name and the closing.

- The **business letter** format is used for most letters not sent to friends or relatives.

Practice

Directions: Draft a business letter requesting an interview with someone you admire.

_____

_____

_____

_____

_____

_____

_____

_____

On Your Own: Revise, polish, and send your request. You never know—you might get the interview if you list enough good reasons!

Name: _____ Date: _____

Unit 1: Writing a Personal Letter

Key Ideas

- A **personal letter** is one that is written to a friend or a relative.

- A **personal letter** is similar to a business letter, except in the following ways:
  - There is no inside address.
  - There is a comma rather than a colon after the salutation.
  - The salutation and closing are more casual:
    Examples: Hi, Sam,   With love,
    Yo, Tom,   Your bud,

- A **personal letter** is best when it sounds conversational—as if you are talking to someone in person.

Practice

Directions: Write a personal letter that advises and persuades a friend to make a change in his/her life. Use your own paper if you need more room.

_____

_____

_____

_____

_____

_____

_____

_____

_____

_____

_____

On Your Own: Revise, polish, and send your letter, if you wish.

Name: _____ Date: _____

Unit 1: Writing an E-mail

Key Ideas

- Electronic mail (**e-mail**) can be used to send business letters or social letters.

- **E-mail** messages are typically direct and shorter than regular letters.

- Rules for **e-mail** are:
  - Your message should be short and to the point.
  - Never use all capital letters—this is considered shouting online.
  - Always spell check your e-mail and proofread for errors.
  - Use basic letter-writing format: date, greeting, body of message, closing, and signature.
  - Always capitalize the beginning of your sentences, and use appropriate punctuation.

Practice

Directions: Pretend that a good friend or relative asked you what you would consider to be the best birthday present ever. Respond to his/her question by e-mail. Review the rules for e-mail above.

From: **To:** **Subject:** **Date:**

On Your Own: Observe the e-mail you get regularly. How often are the rules violated? Can you edit the mistakes? Observe your own e-mail, and edit your mistakes too.

Name: _____ Date: _____

Unit 1: Chatting on the Internet

Key Ideas

- **Message boards** are ways to stimulate ongoing conversations with a group of friends or like-minded people.

- **Message boards** do not depend on people being online at the time a message is posted and are available 24 hours a day.

- **E-Board** etiquette includes:
  - Sharing only what you want to. Because it is easier to share things when not face-to-face, e-boarders sometimes share more than they should!
  - Remembering where you are; sometimes people develop real relationships and forget they are in cyberspace and not in a real room! Be careful.
  - Count to ten ... there will be negative, pessimistic people in chat rooms just as there are in real life; try not to jump to conclusions. Maybe the person is just having a bad day.
  - Get the most out of it you can; if you need help, ask. Everyone was new to chat rooms (and e-boards) at one time.
  - Abbreviate to save time.
  - Use emoticons—those little pictures made with type characters :)—to show how you feel.

Practice

Directions: Set up a message board for your classroom using paper and pencil and a bulletin board. Use standard e-board etiquette. Ask one of the following questions and have class members respond to it.

1. When was the last time you really laughed at yourself because you did something silly?

2. Of all the nice things someone could truthfully say about you, which one would make you feel the best?

3. Are you in a hurry to grow up? What does it mean to be a "grown-up," and when do you think it will happen to you?

Once you understand the idea of a message board, ask your computer teacher to set up an electronic bulletin board for classroom use. Try it out!

On Your Own: With your parents' permission, participate in a kids' message board to discuss issues of current interest.

11

Name: _____ Date: _____

Unit 1: Writing a Message

Key Ideas

- The purpose of writing a **message** to someone is to inform them of something.

- It is important when writing a **message** that you use clear, concise language.

- When writing a **message**, it is important that you separate main ideas from details.

Practice

Directions: With a partner, and using the form below, take a detailed message in which he/she gives you directions to his/her house.

IMPORTANT MESSAGE

Time/Date:	Taken By:

For:

From:

Telephone:
(   )

- ☐ Telephoned
- ☐ Wants to see you
- ☐ Returned your call
- ☐ Was here to see you

- ☐ Please call
- ☐ Will call again
- ☐ URGENT

_____

_____

_____

_____

_____

On Your Own: Practice taking good telephone messages at home. Be sure they are complete. See if anyone in your house notices!

Name: _____ Date: _____

Unit 1: Filling Out a Form

Key Ideas

- **Forms** are sometimes used to gather information. Different **forms** require different information.

- Always check with a parent, guardian, or teacher before providing any information on a **form**.

- It is most important to proofread the **form** to make sure the information you give is correct.

Practice

Directions: Complete and proofread this sample form for a bank account:

AC Name 1 AC Name 2				AC #	

NAME 1

SS #		DOB		Mother's Maiden Name	
Street Address					Hold ☐
City	State	Zip	Home Phone		Address Verified ☐
No. Years at Above Address		Mortgage Holder or Landholder			
Previous Address (if less than 3 years)					No. Years
ID Type				Issue Date	
Expiration Date			Card No.		
Employed By				Verified	No. Years
Employer Address				Business Phone	

NAME 2

SS #		DOB		Mother's Maiden Name	
Street Address					Hold ☐
City	State	Zip	Home Phone		Address Verified ☐
No. Years at Above Address		Mortgage Holder or Landholder			
Previous Address (if less than 3 years)					No. Years
ID Type				Issue Date	
Expiration Date			Card No.		
Employed By				Verified	No. Years
Employer Address				Business Phone	

On Your Own: In a small group, brainstorm ideas for a new school club or organization. Create a form for your classmates to fill out in order to join the new club. Revise and proof your form before presenting it to the class.

Unit 1: Writing Skills Test

Directions: Darken the circle next to the choice that is the <u>best</u> answer.

1. When writing to express ideas, it is <u>most</u> important to know which *one* of these?
   - ○ A. Who your audience is
   - ○ B. What your supporting sentences are
   - ○ C. What your closing is going to be
   - ○ D. How old you are

2. When writing to express ideas, it is also important to know which *one* of these?
   - ○ A. How to write paragraphs
   - ○ B. How to write a complete sentence
   - ○ C. What your purpose is
   - ○ D. What your title is going to be

3. Finally, when writing to express ideas, it is <u>most</u> important to know which *one* of these?
   - ○ A. The writing format you need
   - ○ B. What you want to say
   - ○ C. What you enjoy about writing
   - ○ D. How long it will take you to write

4. Which of these <u>best</u> describes the purpose of *letter writing*?
   - ○ A. To tell a true story that happened to the person who tells it
   - ○ B. To create a written conversation between teacher and student
   - ○ C. To record private thoughts and ideas
   - ○ D. To keep in touch with friends and relatives

5. Which of these <u>best</u> describes a *dialogue journal*?
   - ○ A. A true story that happened to the person who tells it
   - ○ B. A written conversation between teacher and student
   - ○ C. A record of private thoughts and ideas
   - ○ D. A way to keep in touch with friends and relatives

6. Which of these <u>best</u> describes a *business letter*?
   - ○ A. A letter format used for most letters not sent to friends or relatives
   - ○ B. A conversational letter written to a friend or relative
   - ○ C. Electronic mail used for business or social reasons
   - ○ D. An electronic conversation between several people simultaneously

7. Which one of these <u>best</u> describes a *personal letter*?
   - ○ A. A letter format used for most letters not sent to friends or relatives
   - ○ B. A conversational letter written to a friend or relative
   - ○ C. Electronic mail used for business or social reasons
   - ○ D. An electronic conversation between several people simultaneously

8. Which of these <u>best</u> describes an *electronic message board*?
   - ○ A. A letter format used for most letters not sent to friends or relatives
   - ○ B. A conversational letter written to a friend or relative
   - ○ C. Electronic mail used for business or social reasons
   - ○ D. An electronic conversation between several people simultaneously

Name: _____ Date: _____

Unit 1: Writing Skills Test (cont.)

9. Which of these <u>best</u> describes an *e-mail message*?
   - ○ A. A letter format used for most letters not sent to friends or relatives
   - ○ B. A conversational letter written to a friend or relative
   - ○ C. Electronic mail used for business or social reasons
   - ○ D. An electronic conversation between several people simultaneously

10. Which of these <u>best</u> describes the purpose of *writing a message*?
    - ○ A. To gather important information
    - ○ B. To communicate with friends or relatives
    - ○ C. To inform someone of something
    - ○ D. To record private thoughts and ideas

11. Which of these <u>best</u> describes the purpose of *filling out a form*?
    - ○ A. To gather important information
    - ○ B. To communicate with friends or relatives
    - ○ C. To inform someone of something
    - ○ D. To record private thoughts and ideas

12. Which of these <u>best</u> describes the purpose of keeping a *personal journal*?
    - ○ A. To gather important information
    - ○ B. To communicate with friends or relatives
    - ○ C. To inform someone of something
    - ○ D. To record private thoughts and ideas

13. Which of these is <u>not</u> related to ideas in writing?
    - ○ A. Writing must be clear and make sense.
    - ○ B. The topic must be manageable for the writer.
    - ○ C. There must be important, interesting details.
    - ○ D. The writing must be easy to read aloud.

14. All but one of these is important to ideas in writing. Which one is <u>not</u>?
    - ○ A. Have a clear and interesting topic.
    - ○ B. Show things happening rather than telling about them happening.
    - ○ C. Sentences should be concise, not wordy.
    - ○ D. All important events are included in the order of their happening.

15. The steps in the writing process include all but which one of the following?
    - ○ A. Prewriting
    - ○ B. Word Choice
    - ○ C. Drafting
    - ○ D. Revising
    - ○ E. Editing
    - ○ F. Publishing

Name: _____ Date: _____

Unit 1: Writing Skills Test (cont.)

16.–20.   Writing Sample: **Over the Hill**

- Write a personal journal entry on this topic: What is old to you? Why?

- Before you begin writing, use scratch paper to brainstorm and organize your ideas. Use the best English you can, but do not worry about mistakes. The most important thing is to be clear so that the person reading your writing can understand your ideas and your reasons for those ideas.

- Before time is called, look over your writing to see if the content is focused, original, and interesting. This is the criteria on which you will be evaluated.

_____

_____

_____

_____

_____

_____

_____

_____

_____

_____

_____

_____

_____

_____

_____

_____

Unit 2: Descriptive Writing

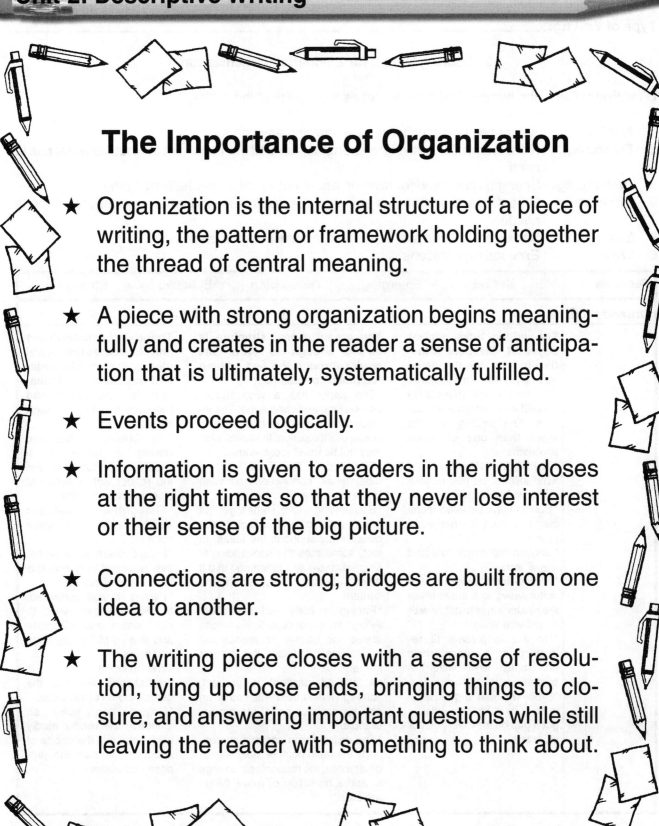

The Importance of Organization

★ Organization is the internal structure of a piece of writing, the pattern or framework holding together the thread of central meaning.

★ A piece with strong organization begins meaningfully and creates in the reader a sense of anticipation that is ultimately, systematically fulfilled.

★ Events proceed logically.

★ Information is given to readers in the right doses at the right times so that they never lose interest or their sense of the big picture.

★ Connections are strong; bridges are built from one idea to another.

★ The writing piece closes with a sense of resolution, tying up loose ends, bringing things to closure, and answering important questions while still leaving the reader with something to think about.

Used with permission from the
Northwest Regional Educational Laboratory (NWREL).

Name: _____ Date: _____

Topic: _____

Type of Writing: _____

2. Scoring Rubric for Evaluating Organization

Directions: Circle the number that best describes the quality of the writing.

1 **Not Yet:**   A bare beginning; writer not yet showing any control
2 **Emerging:**   Need for revision outweighs strengths; isolated moments hint at what the writer has in mind
3 **Developing:**   Strengths and need for revision are about equal; about halfway home
4 **Effective:**   On balance, the strengths outweigh the weaknesses; a small amount of revision is needed
5 **Strong:**   Shows control and skill in this trait; many strengths present
6 **Wow!**   Exceeds expectations

Features	Not Yet	Emerging	Developing	Effective	Strong
Organization:	**1**	**2**	**3**	**4**	**5**
	The writing lacks a clear sense of direction. Ideas, details, or events seem strung together in a loose or random fashion; there is no identifiable internal structure. The writing reflects more than one of these problems: *There is no real lead to set up what follows, no real conclusion to wrap things up. *Connections between ideas are confusing or not even present. *Sequencing needs lots and lots of work. *Pacing feels awkward; the writer slows to a crawl when the reader wants to get on with it, and vice versa. *No title is present (if requested) or, if present, does not match well with the content. *Problems with organization make it hard for the reader to get a grip on the main point or story line.	**The organizational structure is strong enough to move the reader through the text without too much confusion.** *The paper has a recognizable introduction and conclusion. The introduction may not create a strong sense of anticipation; the conclusion may not tie up all loose ends. *Transitions often work well; at other times, connections between ideas are fuzzy. *Sequencing shows some logic, but is not under control enough that it consistently supports the ideas. In fact, sometimes the sequencing is so predictable and rehearsed that it takes attention away from the content. *Pacing is fairly well controlled, though the writer sometimes lunges ahead too quickly or spends too much time on details that do not matter. *A title (if desired) is present, although it may be uninspired or an obvious restatement of the prompt or topic. *The organization sometimes supports the main point or story line; at other times, the reader feels an urge to add a transition or move things around.	**The organization enhances and showcases the central idea or theme. The order and structure of information is compelling and moves the reader through the text.** *An inviting introduction draws the reader in; a satisfying conclusion leaves the reader with a sense of closure and resolution. *Thoughtful transitions clearly show how ideas connect. *Details seem to fit where they're placed; sequencing is logical and effective. *Pacing is well controlled; the writer knows when to slow down and elaborate and when to pick up the pace and move on. *The title, if desired, is original and captures the central theme of the piece. *Organization flows so smoothly the reader hardly thinks about it; the choice of structure matches the purpose and audience.

Comments: _____

Used with permission from the Northwest Regional Educational Laboratory (NWREL).

Name: _____ Date: _____

Unit 2: Student Writing Rubric—Organization

Topic: _____

Type of Writing: *Expository*   *Persuasive*   *Narrative*

Directions: Check those statements that apply to your writing.

_____   I have a clear and interesting topic.

_____   My beginning "grabs" my readers' attention and makes them want to read more.

_____   My writing is easy to follow. Each point leads to the next point.

_____   I include all important events in the order of their happening.

_____   My details add to the story and make it more colorful and interesting.

_____   I *show* things happening rather than *telling* about them.

_____   I include dialogue when appropriate.

_____   I have a strong ending that leaves my readers satisfied.

_____   My ending tells how the story worked out or how I felt about it.

_____   There aren't any important unanswered questions in my story.

Comments: _____

_____

_____

_____

_____

_____

Name: _____ Date: _____

Unit 2: Writing a Description 1

Key Ideas

- Writing a **description** means creating a clear image of a particular thing or person in the reader's mind. The reader can picture the object's size and shape and know what makes it special.

- When writing a **description**, it is important to identify the significant attributes of an object in order to write a vivid description.

- When crafting a **description**, it is important to group details in a logical order.

Practice

Directions: Write a description of a significant object in your life. Suppose your house caught on fire. What is the one thing (not person) you would rescue? Why?

1. Begin by deciding on the object you wish to describe: _____

_____

2. Now concentrate on the sensory details that characterize the object:

Smell	
Sight	
Taste	
Sound	
Touch	

Name: _____ Date: _____

Unit 2: Writing a Description 1 (cont.)

3. You are ready to write your first draft of the description. Do so on the lines below. Then share with someone and ask your partner if he/she formulated a visual image in his/her mind of your object. With your partner, discuss what you might do to make your writing more descriptive.

_____

_____

_____

_____

_____

_____

_____

_____

_____

_____

_____

_____

4. Revise, edit, and write (or type) your final description on good paper. Be sure to give it a catchy title. Write a few possible titles here. Decide which one you like best.

a. _____

b. _____

c. _____

On Your Own: Practice your descriptive writing by describing any of the following: a favorite childhood toy, a childhood treasure, a special place, or an imaginary place in your mind.

Name: _____ Date: _____

Unit 2: Writing a Description 2

Key Ideas

- Writing a **description** means creating a clear image of a particular place in the reader's mind. The reader can get a clear image of what the writer is describing.

- When writing a **description**, it is important to identify the significant attributes of the scene in order to write a vivid description.

- When writing a **description**, it is important to organize the description so that it is logical and helpful to the reader.

Practice

Directions: Describe a place that is very familiar to your classmates. Do not **tell** where or what the place is, but write so that your writing **shows** what the place is like. If you do it well, your classmates should be able to guess what you are describing.

Suggestions: the food court at the mall   the football stadium
                    a particular room in the school   a church, temple, or synagogue
                    a sports event   the school bus

After you have decided on the place you will describe, follow the steps below:

1. If you were in the place you are describing, what would you be seeing, hearing, smelling, tasting, and feeling? Fill in the chart below.

Sights:
Sounds:
Tastes:
Smells:
Textures:

Name: _____ Date: _____

Unit 2: Writing a Description 2 (cont.)

2. Think about how you will **show** the things you have decided to include in your description. Will you include dialogue? How could you do that?

_____

_____

_____

_____

3. Ready to write? Write your first draft here. Don't worry about grammar and spelling right now. The purpose of the first draft is to get your ideas down on paper. Use your notes on the previous page to help you organize your description.

_____

_____

_____

_____

_____

_____

_____

_____

_____

_____

4. Exchange papers with a writing partner. Do the following with each other's descriptions:
   a. Read the paper carefully.
   b. Find a place that **shows** well. Underline the passage or sentence.
   c. Find a place where the paper **tells** rather than **shows**. Put a circle around this section.
   d. Return the paper to the writer.

5. Rewrite, edit, and polish your paper for publication.

23

Name: _____ Date: _____

Unit 2: Writing a Descriptive Paragraph

Key Ideas

- A **descriptive paragraph** tells about one specific topic. The topic should be narrow enough to describe in a handful of sentences.

- A **descriptive paragraph** contains a title, a topic sentence, and sensory details that appeal to all the senses: sight, hearing, smell, touch, and taste.

Practice

Directions: Your task is to draft a good descriptive paragraph of your bedroom that presents a clear visual image in the mind of your reader.

1. Begin by working on a good topic sentence. A **topic sentence** tells what the paragraph is about and has two purposes:

   a. It helps the readers by telling them what the paragraph is about.

   b. It helps the writer focus attention on the main subject and keeps the writer from getting off the topic.

A good topic sentence:

✓ grabs the reader's attention right away.
✓ might start with an interesting question.
✓ might make a statement that surprises the reader.
✓ might start with a dialogue.

_____

_____

_____

_____

_____

_____

_____

Name: _____ Date: _____

Unit 2: Writing a Descriptive Paragraph (cont.)

2. Now brainstorm the *sensory details* that describe your room. Close your eyes and imagine that you are in your bedroom. What words describe:

   the smells: _____

   _____

   the sights: _____

   _____

   the sounds: _____

   _____

   the texture: _____

   _____

   the tastes: _____

   _____

3. Now you are ready to draft your descriptive paragraph about your bedroom:

   _____

   _____

   _____

   _____

   _____

   _____

   _____

   _____

   _____

   _____

On Your Own: Polish and publish your paragraph in a class book. Choose prize categories for nicest room, worst room, most descriptive room, smelliest room, room you would most want to live in, etc. Then have a class vote and award paper blue ribbons.

Name: _____ Date: _____

Unit 2: Writing a Descriptive Essay

Key Ideas

- A **descriptive essay** is a longer piece of writing that brings its topic to life with colorful and precise language, sensory details, and striking comparisons.

- A **descriptive essay** should create a dominant impression of a person, place, or thing through the use of vivid language organized so the reader can also see or experience the thing described.

- An **essay** is organized like a paragraph in that it has a **beginning**, a **middle**, and a **conclusion**.

Practice

Directions: Write a descriptive essay on the most impressive movie villain you have ever seen. Follow the steps below to help you organize your essay.

1. The beginning or introductory paragraph tells who your essay is about and why. Like all great beginnings, it should "grab" your reader's attention right from the very beginning. Remember what you've learned about good beginnings.

> **A good topic sentence:**
>
> ✓ grabs the reader's attention right away.
> ✓ might start with an interesting question.
> ✓ might make a statement that surprises the reader.
> ✓ might start with a dialogue.

Write a beginning paragraph for your essay on the most impressive movie villain you've seen.

_____

_____

_____

_____

_____

_____

Name: _____ Date: _____

Unit 2: Writing a Descriptive Essay (cont.)

2. The middle paragraphs describe and provide detail about the topic introduced in the first paragraph. You are going to have two middle paragraphs: a) one where you describe in great detail the villain; and b) one where you discuss your reasons for choosing this villain as the most impressive.

   Write a paragraph where you describe in vivid detail your movie villain.

   _____

   _____

   _____

   _____

   Write a second paragraph where you discuss your reasons for choosing your villain as the most impressive movie villain of all time.

   _____

   _____

   _____

3. The final paragraph concludes and sums up the topic. A strong ending makes the essay feel finished.

   Write a final paragraph to conclude and sum up your essay on the most impressive movie villain.

   _____

   _____

   _____

   _____

4. Now, put it all together and write your first draft of the essay on your own paper. Reread it aloud, listening for places that need to be reworked. Is there enough description?

5. Think of a good title for your essay. Draft a few and see which one works best.

   a. _____

   b. _____

6. Share your draft with a writing partner, revise, edit, and polish for publication.

Name: _____ Date: _____

Unit 2: Writing a Character Sketch

Key Ideas

- A **character sketch** is a descriptive piece of writing that focuses on a dominant impression of a person.

- A **character sketch** should use lively details and exact language to support this impression.

- A **character sketch** should conclude with a strong summarizing idea.

Practice

Directions: Choose a character who really interests you (e.g., a distant friend, a mysterious stranger, a memorable character from a movie or a book, a well-known person in your city or town, or yourself from another's point of view), and write a character sketch about that person.

1. What is the particular dominant impression of that person that you want to express?

   _____

2. Describe the person's physical characteristics, including clothing, movements, and facial expressions.

   _____

   _____

   _____

   _____

   _____

   _____

3. Relate important facts about your character's past.

   _____

   _____

   _____

   _____

Name: _____ Date: _____

Unit 2: Writing a Character Sketch (cont.)

4. Use the character's own words if these relate to creating the impression of the person you want to create.

   _____

   _____

   _____

5. Describe the character's opinions and typical activities.

   _____

   _____

   _____

   _____

6. Show (don't tell) the character in action by relating a vignette or experience that involved the character.

   _____

   _____

   _____

   _____

7. Describe how others feel about the character.

   _____

   _____

   _____

   _____

8. Now that you have all the information, organize it in such a way that it will help your readers see the character vividly.

9. Read aloud to a partner, revise, edit, and polish.

10. Publish your character sketch with those of your classmates in a class book, *Some Very Interesting Characters.*

On Your Own: If you didn't already do this, try to write a character sketch of yourself as someone else sees you (e.g., mother, father, sibling, friend, teacher).

Name: _____ Date: _____

Unit 2: Writing Skills Test

Directions: Darken the circle next to the choice that is the <u>best</u> answer.

1. When writing for organization, which one of these is <u>most</u> important?
   - ○ A. A clear and interesting topic
   - ○ B. Interesting dialogue
   - ○ C. Giving my opinion
   - ○ D. Adding good description

2. When a piece of writing is well organized,
   - ○ A. it has a strong beginning.
   - ○ B. it has a strong ending.
   - ○ C. it reads well out loud.
   - ○ D. all of the above.

3. When concentrating on the organization of writing, it is important for the writer to
   - ○ A. provide visual illustrations.
   - ○ B. describe where the supplies are.
   - ○ C. include all events in the order of their happening.
   - ○ D. leave unanswered questions to pique the reader's curiosity.

4. Good organization means
   - ○ A. that the paper is clear and interesting.
   - ○ B. the mechanical correctness of the writing is good.
   - ○ C. that the ideas are in a logical order and are tied to one another.
   - ○ D. that the reader can hear the writer's voice.

5. When organizing your writing, it is important to
   - ○ A. have good control over the conventions of writing.
   - ○ B. make connections and build bridges.
   - ○ C. polish it for publication.
   - ○ D. argue on a topic for which the writer feels strongly.

6. Which one of these <u>best</u> describes a good beginning?
   - ○ A. It stays on the topic.
   - ○ B. It uses time clues to help the reader know when things happened.
   - ○ C. It grabs the reader's attention right away.
   - ○ D. It tells the events in the order in which they happened.

7. All but *one* of these describe a good beginning. Which one does <u>not</u>?
   - ○ A. A good beginning might tell the reader what the purpose of the writing is.
   - ○ B. A good beginning might start with an interesting question.
   - ○ C. A good beginning might start with a statement that surprises the reader.
   - ○ D. A good beginning might start with a dialogue.

8. Which of these <u>best</u> describes a strong ending?
   - ○ A. It grabs the reader's attention.
   - ○ B. It includes details that tell what the author saw, heard, or felt.
   - ○ C. It makes use of dialogue when appropriate.
   - ○ D. It makes the narrative feel finished for the reader.

Name: _____ Date: _____

Unit 2: Writing Skills Test (cont.)

9. All but *one* of these describes a strong ending. Which one does <u>not</u>?
   - ○ A. A strong ending may tell how the experience worked out.
   - ○ B. A strong ending may end with the words: THE END.
   - ○ C. A strong ending may tell what the writer thought or felt about the experience.
   - ○ D. A strong ending may elaborate or add details to the story.

10. Which of the following explains the purpose of writing a *description*?
   - ○ A. To create a clear image of a particular thing or person in the reader's mind
   - ○ B. To focus on a dominant impression of a person
   - ○ C. To create a longer piece of writing that brings its topic to life with colorful and precise language, sensory details, and striking comparisons
   - ○ D. To tell about a specific topic narrow enough to describe in a handful of sentences

11. Which of the following is the purpose of writing a *descriptive paragraph*?
   - ○ A. To create a clear image of a particular thing or person in the reader's mind
   - ○ B. To focus on a dominant impression of a person
   - ○ C. To create a longer piece of writing that brings its topic to life with colorful and precise language, sensory details, and striking comparisons
   - ○ D. To tell about a specific topic narrow enough to describe in a handful of sentences

12. Which of the following best describes a *descriptive essay*?
   - ○ A. A piece of writing that persuades the reader to change his/her mind
   - ○ B. A piece of writing that focuses on a dominant impression of a person
   - ○ C. A longer piece of writing that brings its topic to life with colorful and precise language, sensory details, and striking comparisons
   - ○ D. A piece of writing that describes a narrow topic in a handful of sentences

13. Which of the following best describes a *character sketch*?
   - ○ A. A piece of writing that persuades the reader to change his/her mind
   - ○ B. A piece of writing that focuses on a dominant impression of a person
   - ○ C. A longer piece of writing that brings its topic to life with colorful and precise language, sensory details, and striking comparisons
   - ○ D. A piece of writing that describes a narrow topic in a handful of sentences

14. When writing a description, it is important to do all but *one* of the following.
   - ○ A. To organize the description so it is logical and helpful to the reader
   - ○ B. To identify the significant attributes of the person, place, or thing being described
   - ○ C. To keep the description short and to the point
   - ○ D. To create a clear image in the reader's mind

15. All but *one* of these describes a good character sketch. Which one does <u>not</u>?
   - ○ A. A character sketch should make a statement that surprises the reader.
   - ○ B. A character sketch should focus on a dominant impression of a person.
   - ○ C. A character sketch should use lively details and exact language for support.
   - ○ D. A character sketch should conclude with a strong summarizing idea.

Name: _____ Date: _____

Unit 2: Writing Skills Test (cont.)

16–20.   Writing sample: **An Overrated (or Underrated) Performer**

- Write a descriptive essay that brings this topic to life with colorful and precise language, sensory details, and striking comparisons. Be sure to organize your essay into a beginning, a middle, and an end.

- Before you begin writing, use scratch paper to organize your ideas. It is important to clearly describe your chosen performer and to discuss your reasons for declaring him/her overrated or underrated.

- Use the best English you can, but do not worry about mistakes. The most important thing is to be clear and organized so the person reading your writing can have a visual image of that person and a clear understanding of your position on the topic.

_____

_____

_____

_____

_____

_____

_____

_____

_____

_____

_____

_____

Unit 3: Persuasive Writing

The Importance of Voice

★ Voice is the writer coming through the words, the sense that a real person is speaking and cares about the message.

★ Voice is the personal tone and flavor of the writer's message, the magic, the wit, the feeling, the life and breath.

★ The writer's voice is unmistakably his or hers alone. When the writer is engaged personally with the topic, his or her unique perspective is imparted through the piece.

★ The writer's voice should fit the audience and the purpose for writing.

★ Voice in a narrative story is often different from the voice in an expository essay; however, both voices can be powerful and compelling.

Name: _____ Date: _____

Topic: _____

Type of Writing: _____

3. Scoring Rubric for Evaluating Voice

Directions: Circle the number that best describes the quality of the writing.

1 **Not Yet:**   A bare beginning; writer not yet showing any control
2 **Emerging:**   Need for revision outweighs strengths; isolated moments hint at what the writer has in mind
3 **Developing:** Strengths and need for revision are about equal; about halfway home
4 **Effective:** On balance, the strengths outweigh the weaknesses; a small amount of revision is needed
5 **Strong:**   Shows control and skill in this trait; many strengths present
6 **Wow!**   Exceeds expectations

Features	Not Yet	Emerging	Developing	Effective	Strong
Voice:	**1**	**2**	**3**	**4**	**5**
	The writer seems indifferent, uninvolved, or distanced from the topic and/or the audience. As a result, the paper reflects more than one of the following problems: *The writer is not concerned with the audience. The writer's style is a complete mismatch for the intended reader or the writing is so short that little is accomplished beyond introducing the topic. *The writer speaks in a kind of monotone that flattens all potential highs or lows of the message. *The writing is humdrum and "risk-free." *The writing is lifeless or mechanical; depending on the topic, it may be overly technical or jargonistic. *The development of the topic is so limited that no point of view is present.		**The writer seems sincere but not fully engaged or involved. The result is pleasant or even personable, but not compelling.** *The writer seems aware of an audience but discards personal insights in favor of obvious generalities. *The writing communicates in an earnest, pleasing, yet safe manner. *Only one or two moments here or there intrigue, delight, or move the reader. These places may emerge strongly for a line or two, but quickly fade away. *Expository or persuasive writing lacks consistent engagement with the topic to build credibility. *Narrative writing is reasonably sincere, but doesn't reflect a unique or individual perspective about the topic.		**The writer speaks directly to the reader in a way that is individual, compelling, and engaging. The writer crafts the writing with an awareness and respect for the audience and the purpose for writing.** *The tone of the writing adds interest to the message and is appropriate for the purpose and audience. *The reader feels a strong interaction with the writer, sensing the person behind the words. *The writer takes a risk by revealing who he or she is consistently throughout the piece. *Expository or persuasive writing reflects a strong commitment to the topic by showing why the reader needs to know this and why he or she should care. *Narrative writing is honest, personal, and engaging, and makes you think about and react to the author's ideas and point of view.

Comments: _____

Used with permission from the
Northwest Regional Educational Laboratory (NWREL).

Unit 3: Student Writing Rubric—Voice

Topic: _____

Type of Writing: *Expository*   *Persuasive*   *Narrative*

Directions: Check those statements that apply to your writing.

_____   I have a clear and interesting topic.

_____   The reader can tell I like this topic.

_____   My writing has pizazz, spark, and personality.

_____   My writing has energy, enthusiasm, and confidence.

_____   My writing sounds like me.

_____   I am open and honest about my topic.

_____   My language is appropriate to my topic and my audience.

_____   I use dialogue in a natural way.

_____   My story reads well out loud.

_____   My writing reaches out to "grab" my reader's attention and holds it right up to the end.

Comments: _____

_____

_____

_____

_____

_____

_____

Name: _____   Date: _____

Unit 3: Writing With Voice

Key Ideas

- Your **voice** puts your personal imprint on your writing.

- **Voice** means choosing strong, expressive words for your writing.

- **Voice** means using descriptive language and details to show your feelings and your opinions.

- Writers let their **voice** come through their writing by using familiar words that say just what they mean.

Practice

Directions: Practice writing with voice by completing the exercises below.

Example: Sentence: My grandparents are coming.
         Why?   My grandparents are coming for the holiday.
         How?   My grandparents are flying in from Florida for the holiday.
         Where?   My grandparents are flying in to Metro from their home in Tampa, Florida, to spend the holiday with us.
         When?   Next Sunday, my grandparents are flying in from their home in Tampa, Florida, to spend the holiday with us.

Now you try:

1. The boat was sunk.
   How? _____
   _____
   When? _____
   _____
   Why? _____
   _____
   Where? _____
   _____

2. The wind began to blow.
   How? _____
   _____
   When? _____
   _____
   Why? _____
   _____
   Where? _____
   _____

3. The airplane landed.
   How? _____
   _____
   When? _____
   _____
   Why? _____
   _____
   Where? _____
   _____

4. Close the door.
   How? _____
   _____
   When? _____
   _____
   Why? _____
   _____
   Where? _____
   _____

On Your Own: Practice choosing interesting words to "punch up" your writing. Avoid overly-difficult language, however.

Name: _____ Date: _____

Unit 3: Writing a Persuasive Paragraph

Key Ideas

- A **persuasive paragraph** is a paragraph in which the writer attempts to convince the reader to accept his/her point of view.

- A **persuasive paragraph** should provide convincing evidence arranged in a logical order.

- A **persuasive paragraph** should use convincing but reasonable language and should be written in a strong voice (i.e., the "voice" of the writer should come through the writing).

Practice

Directions: Think of something that your town/city needs. Then write a persuasive paragraph that attempts to convince your readers (your peers) to accept your point of view.

1. What is it that your town/city needs? _____

   _____

2. Why? What reasons do you have for wanting/needing this? _____

   _____

   _____

   _____

   _____

3. Now design a good topic sentence for your paragraph. Remember, a topic sentence tells what the paragraph is about and has two purposes:
   a. It helps the reader by telling him/her what the paragraph is about;
   b. It helps the writer focus attention on the main subject and keeps the writer from getting off topic.

A good topic sentence grabs the reader's attention right from the beginning. It might start with an interesting question, make a statement that surprises the reader, or begin with dialogue.

   _____

   _____

   _____

   _____

Name: _____ Date: _____

Unit 3: Writing a Persuasive Paragraph (cont.)

4. The next handful of sentences (your middle) contains the "evidence" for your position. Look back at your answers to #2. Expand and rewrite so it sounds like you are arguing your position; don't use "informal" language, however.

_____

_____

_____

_____

_____

_____

_____

5. Writing a strong ending is as important as writing a strong beginning. A strong ending concludes or sums up the topic. It makes the paragraph feel "finished" for the reader. It does not introduce new information or new arguments; it summarizes arguments and information already made. Write a final sentence that concludes your paragraph.

_____

_____

_____

6. Put the parts together and rewrite your paragraph. Read it aloud to someone else. Ask how you might make it better. Rewrite and edit. Fix the parts that do not read well aloud.

7. Draft at least two good titles for your paragraph. Then choose the one you like best.

    a. _____

    b. _____

8. Read your paragraph to others. See if you can get them to agree with you. If they do, have them sign their names to your paragraph. Each person, however, can only sign two papers other than his or her own.

On Your Own: If your "issue" is a popular one, consider rewriting your paragraph as a letter to your town/city council or a letter to the editor of the local newspaper.

Name: _____ Date: _____

Unit 3: Writing a Persuasive Essay

Key Ideas

- A **persuasive essay** is an essay in which the writer argues on a topic he/she has strong beliefs about; a **persuasive essay** is longer than a persuasive paragraph.

- In a **persuasive essay**, the writer introduces his/her argument, presents supporting reasons, draws conclusions, and convinces the reader to accept the writer's viewpoint.

- A great **persuasive essay** has the following characteristics:
  - a clear statement of the writer's position, what he/she wants the reader to believe,
  - at least three strong reasons that support the argument,
  - elaboration of each argument with facts and examples,
  - convincing language that is both positive and polite,
  - clear organization that best persuades the reader, and
  - a summarization of the argument and reasons at the end of the essay.

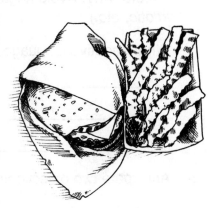

Practice

Directions: Using the questions below to help organize your thoughts, write a persuasive essay on the following topic:

Should middle-school students be allowed to leave the school campus for lunch?

1. Which side of the argument are you on? _____

    _____

2. Why? List at least three reasons (with examples) for your opinion.

    a. _____

       _____

    b. _____

       _____

    c. _____

       _____

    Are any of these reasons weak? Can you replace it with a stronger reason?

    _____

    _____

Name: _____ Date: _____

Unit 3: Writing a Persuasive Essay (cont.)

3. Order your reasons by importance. Most important should be #1.

   #1 _____ #2 _____ #3 _____

4. Use persuasive, positive language (e.g., *obviously, clearly, definitely,* etc.), and write in a forceful way. Avoid negative, loaded language and name-calling (e.g., *crazy, ridiculous, idiotic,* etc.).

   What negative language have you used? _____

   _____

   _____

   _____

5. Anticipate two objections to your opinion that an opponent might raise:

   _____

   _____

   _____

   _____

   _____

   _____

6. What answers do you have to these objections?

   _____

   _____

   _____

   _____

   _____

   _____

7. Draft your persuasive essay. Remember, it is only a draft. Don't be too concerned about spelling and grammar; the important point here is to get your ideas down on paper.

Name: _____ Date: _____

Unit 3: Writing a Book Review

Key Ideas

- A **book review** is a piece of writing in which the writer shares his/her opinion about the book, discusses details from the book that support his/her opinion, and makes a recommendation to others.

- A **book review** follows the format for an essay and includes:
  - a **title** that informs;
  - an **introduction** with a thesis statement;
  - the **body** of the essay;
  - the **conclusion**.

- All parts of the **book review** must work together to present and develop the writer's opinion.

Practice

Directions: Topic: Reporting on a historical novel

Task: Write a book review of a historical novel that informs, evaluates, and persuades a reader to read the historical novel.

1. Choose your book. A historical novel is one that takes place sometime in the past. Read the book and take notes on important parts.

2. Draft a sentence that clearly states, in a strong voice, your opinion of the book.

   _____

   _____

   _____

3. Note the pages and passages in the book that you may use to support your opinion.

   _____

   _____

   _____

4. Draft a sentence that clearly states, in strong language, your recommendation of the book.

   _____

   _____

   _____

Name: _____ Date: _____

Unit 3: Writing a Book Review (cont.)

5. Now work on your thesis statement. A thesis statement is a complete sentence that tells exactly what you are trying to persuade your readers to believe and why. It is much like a topic sentence in a paragraph. Try writing a thesis statement for your book review.

    _____

    _____

    _____

6. Expand your thesis statement into a handful of sentences to make up your beginning paragraph. Can you make your beginning more interesting? Are you convincing? Does your voice come through?

    _____

    _____

    _____

    _____

7. The middle paragraphs (or body) of the book review develop the thesis statement and discuss the details from the book that support your opinion (without giving away the ending of the book). Draft your middle paragraphs here.

    _____

    _____

    _____

    _____

    _____

8. Lastly, the final paragraph will conclude and sum up the thesis statement AND make a recommendation to others (for or against) in three or four sentences. Write your final paragraph below.

    _____

    _____

    _____

    _____

9. When your book review is as good as you can make it, make a good copy for publication.

Name: _____ Date: _____

Unit 3: Writing a Movie or TV Review

Key Ideas

- A **movie or TV review** is a piece of writing in which the writer shares his/her opinion about the movie or TV show, discusses details from the movie or TV show that support his/her opinion, and makes a recommendation to others.

- A good **movie or TV review** tells what to expect without giving everything away.

- A **movie or TV review** follows the format of an essay in that it has an interesting **beginning** that includes a good thesis statement, a **body** that includes the details or evidence that supports the writer's opinion, and a strong **ending**.

Practice

Directions: Write a review of a current movie or TV show that you have seen but many others haven't.

1. Choose your movie or TV show. Why did you choose this one? _____

_____

2. The beginning or introductory paragraph does two things: it must grab the reader's attention, and it tells the reader what the point of your review is (your opinion of the movie or TV show).

   Remember what you've learned about good beginnings:

A good topic sentence:
✓ grabs the reader's attention right away.
✓ might start with an interesting question.
✓ might make a statement that surprises the reader.
✓ might start with a dialogue.

   Write a beginning paragraph for your movie or TV review. The first sentence is often the most important sentence.

   _____

   _____

   _____

   _____

Name: _____ Date: _____

Unit 3: Writing a Movie or TV Review (cont.)

3. The middle paragraphs are where the writer discusses details from the movie or TV show (without giving too much away) and presents evidence to support his/her viewpoint.

   Draft the middle (or body) of your review here.

   _____

   _____

   _____

   _____

   _____

   _____

   _____

   _____

4. The final paragraph concludes and sums up the topic and makes a recommendation to readers. A strong ending makes the review feel finished.

   Write a final paragraph to conclude and sum up your movie or TV review.

   _____

   _____

   _____

   _____

5. Now, put it all together and write a first draft of your review. Reread it aloud, looking for places that need to be reworked. Is your voice clear?

6. Think of a good, provocative title for your review. Draft a few and see which one works best.

   a. _____

   b. _____

7. Share your draft with a writing partner, revise, edit, and polish for publication.

Name: _____ Date: _____

Unit 3: Writing Skills Test

Directions: Darken the circle next to the choice that is the <u>best</u> answer.

1. Writing with voice means
   - ○ A. letting the reader's personality come through the writing.
   - ○ B. letting the writer's personality come through the writing.
   - ○ C. letting the writing do the talking.
   - ○ D. letting the writer's words overpower the message.

2. Finding voice in your writing is important because
   - ○ A. it expands and clarifies the reader's ideas
   - ○ B. it makes use of colorful, interesting words.
   - ○ C. it is the heart and soul and the magic of writing.
   - ○ D. it makes it easy to read the writing.

3. When a piece of reading has "voice" it means
   - ○ A. the reader can sense the real person behind the words.
   - ○ B. the reader can sense that the person behind the words believes in those words.
   - ○ C. the reader can sense that the writer really cares about what is being said.
   - ○ D. all of the above.

4. Writing with voice is important in persuasive writing because
   - ○ A. it uses persuasive writing tools effectively.
   - ○ B. it presents strong arguments and opinions.
   - ○ C. it can persuade the reader to change his/her opinion.
   - ○ D. it helps the writer state his/her position clearly.

5. Which of the following are characteristics of voice?
   - ○ A. The writer is open and honest about the topic.
   - ○ B. The writing sounds like the writer talking.
   - ○ C. The reader can tell the writer likes the topic.
   - ○ D. All of the above

6. Which of the following is the purpose of *writing to persuade*?
   - ○ A. To chronicle events in one's life or in the lives of others
   - ○ B. To draw generalizations about life
   - ○ C. To learn and share information
   - ○ D. To convince someone to share or accept the writer's way of thinking

7. Which of these is true of *writing with voice*?
   - ○ A. Writers use familiar words that say just what they mean.
   - ○ B. Writers use big and difficult words to "punch up" their writing.
   - ○ C. Writers use convincing language to persuade the reader.
   - ○ D. Writers use overworked verbs because they are familiar to readers.

Unit 3: Writing Skills Test (cont.)

8. Which of the following <u>best</u> describes a *persuasive paragraph*?
   - ○ A. A piece of writing in which the writer shares his/her opinion about a movie or TV show
   - ○ B. A piece of writing in which the writer shares his/her opinion about a book
   - ○ C. A longer piece of writing in which the writer argues on a topic about which he/she has strong beliefs
   - ○ D. A handful of sentences in which the writer attempts to convince the reader to accept his/her point of view

9. Which of the following <u>best</u> describes a *persuasive essay*?
   - ○ A. A piece of writing in which the writer shares his/her opinion about a movie or TV show
   - ○ B. A piece of writing in which the writer shares his/her opinion about a book
   - ○ C. A longer piece of writing in which the writer argues on a topic about which he/she has strong beliefs
   - ○ D. A handful of sentences in which the writer attempts to convince the reader to accept his/her point of view

10. Which of the following <u>best</u> describes a *book review*?
   - ○ A. A piece of writing in which the writer shares his/her opinion about a movie or TV show
   - ○ B. A piece of writing in which the writer shares his/her opinion about a book
   - ○ C. A longer piece of writing in which the writer argues on a topic about which he/she has strong beliefs
   - ○ D. A handful of sentences in which the writer attempts to convince the reader to accept his/her point of view

11. Which of the following <u>best</u> describes a *movie or TV review*?
   - ○ A. A piece of writing in which the writer shares his/her opinion about a movie or TV show
   - ○ B. A piece of writing in which the writer shares his/her opinion about a book
   - ○ C. A longer piece of writing in which the writer argues on a topic about which he/she has strong beliefs
   - ○ D. A handful of sentences in which the writer attempts to convince the reader to accept his/her point of view

12. Which of these describes the purpose of a *topic sentence*? (There may be more than one.)
   - ○ A. It helps the reader by telling him/her what the paragraph or essay is about.
   - ○ B. It starts with an interesting question for the reader to think about.
   - ○ C. It states the writer's reasons for his/her strong beliefs.
   - ○ D. It helps the writer focus attention on the main subject and keeps the writer from getting off the topic.

Name: _____ Date: _____

Unit 3: Writing Skills Test (cont.)

13. An effective introduction for a persuasive piece of writing may do all but which *one* of the following?
    - ○ A. It asks a question.
    - ○ B. It states a hypothesis.
    - ○ C. It creates a mental image.
    - ○ D. It tells an anecdote.

14. Which of these is not true about a strong ending?
    - ○ A. A strong ending is as important as a strong beginning.
    - ○ B. A strong ending concludes or sums up the topic.
    - ○ C. A strong ending adds one more interesting idea to the topic.
    - ○ D. A strong ending makes the reader feel satisfied.

15. Which of these describes the characteristics of a *persuasive essay*? (There may be more than one.)
    - ○ A. It contains a clear statement of the writer's opinion.
    - ○ B. It has at least three strong reasons that support the writer's argument.
    - ○ C. It elaborates each argument with facts and examples.
    - ○ D. It uses convincing language that is both positive and polite.

Name: _____ Date: _____

Unit 3: Writing Skills Test (cont.)

16.–20.   Writing Sample: **Sex and Violence**

- Should all sex and violence be removed from television? Why or why not? Write a persuasive essay about this topic. Be clear about your position, and support it with reasons and examples.

- Before you begin writing, use scratch paper to organize your ideas. It is most important that you introduce your subject clearly with a good thesis statement, and then present supporting arguments and reasons. End with a strong summarization of your argument.

- Use the best English you can, but do not worry about mistakes. The most important thing is that you convince the reader to agree with your opinion. Your writing will be evaluated especially for voice, so make sure "you" come through your writing.

_____

_____

_____

_____

_____

_____

_____

_____

_____

_____

_____

_____

_____

_____

_____

_____

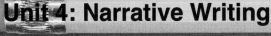

Unit 4: Narrative Writing

The Importance of Word Choice

★ Word choice is the vocabulary that a writer chooses to convey meaning.

★ Good word choice is the use of rich, colorful, precise language that communicates not just in a functional way but in a way that moves and enlightens the reader.

★ Strong word choice in descriptive writing clarifies and expands ideas.

★ Careful word choice in persuasive writing moves the reader to a new vision of things.

★ Strong word choice is characterized not so much by an exceptional vocabulary that impresses the reader, but more by the skill to use everyday words well.

★ Good word choice means using words correctly, with precision and accuracy, and not repetitively.

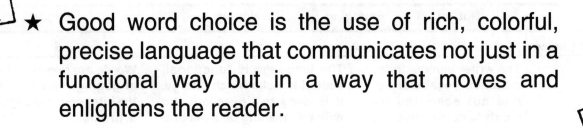

Name: _____ Date: _____

Topic: _____

Type of Writing: _____

4. Scoring Rubric for Evaluating Word Choice

Directions: Circle the number that best describes the quality of the writing.

1 **Not Yet:**   A bare beginning; writer not yet showing any control
2 **Emerging:**   Need for revision outweighs strengths; isolated moments hint at what the writer has in mind
3 **Developing:** Strengths and need for revision are about equal; about halfway home
4 **Effective:**   On balance, the strengths outweigh the weaknesses; a small amount of revision is needed
5 **Strong:**   Shows control and skill in this trait; many strengths present
6 **Wow!**   Exceeds expectations

Features	Not Yet	Emerging	Developing	Effective	Strong
Word Choice:	1	2	3	4	5
	The writer demonstrates a limited vocabulary or has not searched for words to convey specific meaning. *Words are so nonspecific and distracting that only a very limited meaning comes through. *Problems with language leave the reader wondering. Many of the words just don't work in this piece. *Audience has not been considered. Language is used incorrectly, making the message secondary to the misfires with the words. *Limited vocabulary and/or misused parts of speech seriously impair understanding. *Words and phrases are so unimaginative and lifeless that they detract from the meaning. *Jargon or clichés distract or mislead. Redundancy may distract the reader.	**The language is functional, even if it lacks much energy. It is easy to figure out the writer's meaning on a general level.** *Words are adequate and correct in a general sense, and they support the meaning by not getting in the way. *Familiar words and phrases communicate but rarely capture the reader's imagination. *Attempts at colorful language show a willingness to stretch and grow but sometimes reach beyond the audience (thesaurus overload!). *Despite a few successes, the writing is marked by passive verbs, everyday nouns, and mundane modifiers. *The words and phrases are functional with only one or two fine moments. *The words may be refined in a couple of places, but the language looks more like the first thing that popped into the writer's mind.		**Words are powerful and engaging, and convey the intended message in a precise, interesting, and natural way.** *Words are specific and accurate. It is easy to understand just what the writer means. *Striking words and phrases often catch the reader's eye and linger in the reader's mind. *Language and phrasing are natural, effective, and appropriate for the audience. *Lively verbs add energy, while specific nouns and modifiers add depth. *Choices in language enhance the meaning and clarify understanding. *Precision is obvious. The writer has taken care to put just the right word or phrase in just the right spot.

Comments: _____

Name: _____ Date: _____

Unit 4: Student Writing Rubric—Word Choice

Topic: _____

Type of Writing: *Expository*   *Persuasive*   *Narrative*

Directions: Check those statements that apply to your piece of writing.

_____   I have used many interesting words in my writing; I have used words that I *like.*

_____   I chose just the right words to express my ideas and feelings.

_____   I used phrases and words that are colorful and lively.

_____   I chose words that help the reader see, feel, and understand my message.

_____   I have used everyday words well and some everyday words in new and surprising ways.

_____   My words show action, energy, and/or movement.

_____   I used words that clearly convey feelings.

_____   My story reads well out loud.

_____   My readers will be clear about what my words mean.

Comments: _____

_____

_____

_____

_____

_____

_____

_____

Name: _____ Date: _____

Unit 4: Word Choice 1

Key Ideas
- Writers use **well-chosen words** to communicate their message in clear, interesting, precise ways.

- **Word choice** is what gives voice to a piece of writing.

- **Word choice** clarifies and expands the writer's ideas.

Practice

Directions: For each "overused" word below, find at least five more interesting words. Write the new words in the boxes. For example, instead of the word *walk* use *march, stomp, skip, limp,* or another verb that portrays a more exact movement.

1. said   (We said.)

2. sad   (I'm sad.)

3. laughed (She laughed.)

4. nice (He's nice.)

5. saw (I saw it.)

On Your Own: It's good to have your own thesaurus to look up and learn new and more descriptive words. Be a word collector!

52

Name: _____ Date: _____

Unit 4: Word Choice 2

Key Ideas

- One characteristic of good writing is **word choice**. Good writing shows rather than tells.

- Good writers use **detail** that allows a reader to see, hear, and feel what is being described or explained.

    Example 1: She was very dressed up. (This sentence *tells.*)

    Example 2: Her dress was as red as her lips, and it sparkled in the sunlight. There must have been a thousand sequins sewn vertically from neck to hemline. Her pointy-toed, ruby red slippers matched her dress perfectly. In her upswept hair was one perfect, dew-dropped rose that complemented her lightly-applied makeup. She was ready to go to the party. (This description *shows.*)

Practice

Directions: Now you try it. For each of the sentences below, write a passage that *shows* rather than *tells* what the scene is like.

1. The <u>office</u> was a complete <u>mess</u>. (Mention objects in the office that might be part of the mess.)

    _____

    _____

    _____

    _____

2. <u>He</u> <u>started</u> the truck and <u>drove</u> away. (Describe the underlined words in detail.)

    _____

    _____

    _____

    _____

Name: _____ Date: _____

Unit 4: Word Choice 2 (cont.)

3. The <u>child</u> <u>approached</u> the <u>woman</u>. (Describe the underlined words in detail.)

_____

_____

_____

_____

4. The <u>kid</u> <u>left</u> <u>angrily</u>. (Describe the underlined words in detail.)

_____

_____

_____

_____

5. The <u>countryside</u> was <u>beautiful</u>. (Describe the underlined words in detail.)

_____

_____

_____

_____

On Your Own: In your reading, watch for passages that are rich in detail and description. Keep track of any especially good ones, and share them with the class by reading the passage aloud.

Name: _____ Date: _____

Unit 4: Figurative Language

Key Ideas

- **Figurative language** is language used in an unusual or non-literal way, such as in similes or metaphors to create vivid mental images.

    Example: "All the world's a stage."
                        —William Shakespeare
    (metaphor)

- **Similes** compare two things by using the words *like* or *as.*
    Examples: His smile was like the sun on a bright summer morning.
    Her face turned as red as a tomato when he kissed her.

- **Metaphors** say one thing *is* another thing.
    Example: Marcy is a slug bug.
    Bob was the bad apple in the group.

Practice

Directions: Underline the objects being compared in the following sentences. Then decide if the comparison is a simile or a metaphor.

1. She emerged from the beauty salon as fresh as a daisy.

    _____

2. When he lay down, he said the bed was hard as a rock.

    _____

3. My heart is a rainbow of color.

    _____

4. To the lost camper, the gulley was like the Grand Canyon.

    _____

5. The flashlight was a beacon in the night.

    _____

Name: _____ Date: _____

Unit 4: Figurative Language (cont.)

Directions: Finish each sentence below with a simile or a metaphor, and add some descriptive adjectives as well.

6.　The giant stood as tall as _____.

7.　The sun was a _____ in the sky.

8.　Fire engines roared through the night like _____.

9.　Her smile was as bright as _____.

10.　The summer air was a _____.

Directions: For each item, write a sentence using figurative language to describe the image created in your mind. Compare with the type of language shown in parentheses. Consider all the senses—sight, sound, smell, taste, and touch—when creating your sentence.

11.　a boy (simile) _____

12.　a building (metaphor) _____

13.　the autumn leaves (metaphor) _____

14.　the golden retriever's bark (simile) _____

15.　the moon (simile) _____

16.　the ice skater (metaphor) _____

17.　my teacher's voice (simile) _____

18.　his touchdown (simile) _____

19.　our house (metaphor) _____

20.　her heart (simile) _____

21.　the violin (simile) _____

22.　the Venus Flytrap (metaphor) _____

On Your Own: Look for places in your essays where you can use similes and metaphors, and then do it!

Name: _____ Date: _____

Unit 4: Narrative Writing

Key Ideas

- A **narrative** is a series of events told like a story—an account of incidents or events written in story form.

- A **narrative** has the following characteristics:

  - **Title** – hints at what the subject of the narrative is about and tries to attract the reader's attention.
  - **Introduction** – contains the topic of the narrative written in an interesting, informative way in order to "grab" the reader's attention and the thesis statement, which expresses the main idea of the narrative.
  - **Body** – develops the thesis statement with examples, facts, incidents, details, and reasons written in an organized, logical way.
  - **Conclusion** – ends the story with a summary of the thesis statement and the writer's thoughts.

Practice

Directions: Friendship is more than just a word. Write a narrative that relates an experience (a series of events) that conveys an idea about friendship.

1. Think of some experiences from your life that exemplify what friendship means to you. Choose the one that is most interesting to write about. Form your thesis statement here. (*The thesis statement is what you want to say about friendship—written in a complete sentence, of course.)

   _____

   _____

   _____

   _____

   _____

2. List facts, incidents, and details from the experience you are writing about.

   _____

   _____

   _____

   _____

Name: _____ Date: _____

Unit 4: Narrative Writing (cont.)

3. Now think of a good, strong, interesting topic sentence to begin your narrative. Remember to "grab" your reader's attention right from the beginning. (*Topic sentences can begin with a question, a quote, or a surprising statement.)

_____

_____

4. Expand your topic sentence into your introductory paragraph. Remember to include your <u>thesis statement</u>.

_____

_____

_____

_____

5. Organize your thoughts and ideas listed in #2 in some logical fashion, and develop a paragraph for each idea on your own paper.

6. Summarize your main points and restate your <u>thesis statement</u> in your conclusion.

_____

_____

_____

_____

7. Now think of a great title for your narrative. Choose one that will pique your reader's curiosity and make him or her **want** to read your story.

_____

_____

On Your Own: Put the whole narrative together and revise, edit, and polish for publication. Together with your peers, bind the narratives into a book on friendship.

Name: _____ Date: _____

Unit 4: Writing a Personal Narrative

Key Ideas

- A **personal narrative** is a true story about something that happened to the person who tells it.

- **Personal narratives** have certain characteristics.
  - They grab the reader's attention right at the beginning.
  - They are told in first person using the pronoun *I*.
  - They include important events in the order of their happening.
  - They use details to tell what the author saw, heard, or felt.
  - They are told in the author's voice.
  - They have a satisfying ending that tells how the story worked out or how the author felt.

Practice

Directions: Write a personal narrative about a time when you were really happy. Be sure you follow the characteristics listed above.

_____

_____

_____

_____

_____

_____

_____

_____

_____

_____

On Your Own: Write a personal narrative about a favorite childhood toy. Publish the narrative. Maybe you could show the actual toy, if you still have it!

Name: _____ Date: _____

Unit 4: Writing a Narrative Journal

Key Ideas

- **Journal writing** is a way of recording your private thoughts and ideas.

- **Journals** can be private (like a diary) or can be shared with others (like a personal narrative).

- The best **journals** are rich in detail and record what the writer saw, heard, thought, felt, and did.

Practice

Directions: Choose one of the three journal prompts and write about it on the lines below. Choose to keep your journal private, or you may share it with the class.

1. What is the funniest story you ever made up about why you weren't able to get your homework finished on time?
2. If drinking a magic potion would make you never again feel sad no matter what happened, would you drink it?
3. What do your parents do that embarrasses you the most?

_____

_____

_____

_____

_____

_____

_____

_____

_____

_____

On Your Own: Using a special notebook and writing tool, keep a daily journal of your thoughts and opinions. Keep your writing private.

Name: _____ Date: _____

Unit 4: Writing a Memoir

Key Ideas

- A **memoir** is built on the memory of the writer.

- **Memoirs** have the following characteristics:
  - They are told in the first person using the pronoun *I*.
  - They are very descriptive accounts so the reader can experience what the writer experienced.
  - They have well-developed, believable characters.
  - They create details that support the topic even if they aren't "true" to the original memory.
  - They use realistic dialogue to help support the memory and the characters.

- A well-written **memoir** *shows* details of what the writer saw, heard, thought, felt, and did rather than *telling* the reader.

Practice

Directions: Think of a special relative or close friend from the past or present that you share special memories with. Write a memoir of this person.

Memories With a Special Person

1. List ten to 15 memories that you share with this special person.

_____   _____

_____   _____

_____   _____

_____   _____

_____   _____

_____   _____

_____   _____

2. Think about what you've written. What will lend itself to the greatest detail in writing—the most interesting stories? Choose four or five different memories to write about. Put a ✔ before those you plan to use in your memoir.

Name: _____ Date: _____

Unit 4: Writing a Memoir (cont.)

3. Write each memory as a separate paragraph(s). Do not worry about tying them together. Give each memory a title. Write these now. Use your own paper if you need more room.

_____

_____

_____

_____

_____

_____

_____

_____

_____

_____

4. When you are finished writing each memory, go back and read what you've done. Find at least two places in each piece where you are *telling* rather than *showing* or where the description could be expanded. Underline these places. Now rewrite those sections here.

_____

_____

_____

_____

_____

5. Now, put all of the pieces together into your memoir and write a second draft. Exchange with a writing partner and have him/her do what you did in #4. Discuss with each other.

6. Finally, revise, edit, and polish your memoir.

On Your Own: Prepare a copy of your "Memories With a Special Person" for that special person. Give your memoir to him/her as a gift.

Name: _____ Date: _____

Unit 4: Writing an Autobiography

Key Ideas

- An **autobiography** is a history of a person's life written by that person.

- A well-written **autobiography** has detail that *shows* a person's life rather than *telling* about that person's life.

Practice

Directions: Write an autobiographical feature article like those you find in your favorite magazines about people who are featured for something they have accomplished. Use the questions below to help you think, plan, and organize your information.

1. When and where were you born?

   _____

   _____

   What special story or stories are associated with your birth day or date?

   _____

   _____

   What was happening in the world at that time?

   _____

   _____

2. What is your family like, and where are you in the family order?

   _____

   _____

   _____

3. Where do you go (have you gone) to school?

   _____

   _____

Name: _____ Date: _____

Unit 4: Writing an Autobiography (cont.)

4. What are your favorite activities?

_____

_____

_____

5. What do you consider yourself good at or well known for?

_____

_____

_____

6. What are your future hopes and dreams?

_____

_____

_____

7. What do you wish to add to your autobiography?

_____

_____

_____

8. Using the notes you've made above, write the first draft of your autobiography on your own paper.

9. Ask a writing partner to read your autobiography, pointing out any places where you could do a better job of *showing* rather than *telling*.

10. Revise, rewrite, edit, polish, and publish your autobiography. Include a self-portrait, if you wish.

Name: _____ Date: _____

Unit 4: Writing a Historical Narrative

Key Ideas

- A **narrative** is a series of events told like a story; an account of incidents or events written in story form.

- A **narrative** has the following characteristics:

  - **Title** – hints at what the subject of the narrative is about and tries to attract the reader's attention.
  - **Introduction** – contains the topic of the narrative written in an interesting, informative way in order to "grab" the reader's attention and the thesis statement, which expresses the main idea of the narrative.
  - **Body** – develops the thesis statement with examples, facts, incidents, details, and reasons written in an organized, logical way.
  - **Conclusion** – ends the story with a summary of the thesis statement and the writer's thoughts.

Practice

Directions: Write a historical narrative about a significant event in the history of our country. Research your topic and include how this event shaped or changed our country.

_____

_____

_____

_____

_____

_____

_____

_____

On Your Own: Write a narrative about the terrorist attacks of September 11, 2001. How did this affect our nation, and how did it affect you?

Name: _____ Date: _____

Unit 4: Writing a Historical Journal Entry

Key Ideas

- **Journal writing** is a way of recording your private thoughts and ideas.

- **Journals** can be private (like a diary) or can be shared with others (like a personal narrative).

- The best **journals** are rich in detail and record what the writer saw, heard, thought, felt, did, and so on.

Practice

Directions: Invent a journal entry of an eyewitness account to a historical event.

_____

_____

_____

_____

_____

_____

_____

_____

_____

_____

_____

_____

On Your Own: Using a special notebook and writing tool, keep a daily journal of your thoughts and opinions.

Unit 4: Narrative Writing

The Importance of Sentence Fluency

★ Sentence Fluency is the rhythm and flow of the language, the sound of word patterns, the way in which the writing plays to the ear—not just to the eye.

★ The writing is free of awkward word patterns that slow the reader's progress. Sentences are well built and have cadence, power, rhythm, and movement.

★ Sentences vary in length and style, and are so well crafted that reading aloud is a pleasure.

★ Sentences have different beginnings.

★ Complete sentences and fragments express ideas effectively.

Name: _____ Date: _____

Topic: _____

Type of Writing: _____

5. Scoring Rubric for Evaluating Sentence Fluency

Directions: Circle the number that best describes the quality of the writing.

1 **Not Yet:**   A bare beginning; writer not yet showing any control
2 **Emerging:**   Need for revision outweighs strengths; isolated moments hint at what the writer has in mind
3 **Developing:**   Strengths and need for revision are about equal; about halfway home
4 **Effective:**   On balance, the strengths outweigh the weaknesses; a small amount of revision is needed
5 **Strong:**   Shows control and skill in this trait; many strengths present
6 **Wow!**   Exceeds expectations

Features	Not Yet	Emerging	Developing	Effective	Strong
Sentence Fluency:	**1**	**2**	**3**	**4**	**5**
	The reader has to practice quite a bit in order to give this paper a fair interpretive reading. The writing reflects more than one of the following problems: *Sentences are choppy, incomplete, rambling, or awkward; they need work. Phrasing does not sound natural. The patterns may create a singsong rhythm or a chop-chop cadence that lulls the reader to sleep. *There is little or no "sentence sense" present. Even if this piece were flawlessy edited, the sentences would not hang together. *Many sentences begin the same way—and may follow the same patterns (for example, *subject-verb-object*) in a monotonous pattern. *Endless connectives (*and, and so, but then, because, and then,* etc.) or a complete lack of connectives creates a massive jumble of language. *The text does not invite expressive oral reading.		The text hums along with a steady beat but tends to be more pleasant or businesslike than musical, more mechanical than fluid. *Although sentences may not seem artfully crafted or musical, they get the job done in a routine fashion. *Sentences are usually constructed correctly; they hang together; they are sound. *Sentence beginnings are not ALL alike; some variety is attempted. *The reader sometimes has to hunt for clues (for example, connecting words and phrases like *however, therefore, after a while, for example, next, later,* etc.) that show how sentences interrelate. *Parts of the text invite expressive oral reading; others may be stiff, awkward, choppy, or gangly.		The writing has an easy flow, rhythm, and cadence. Sentences are well built, with strong and varied structure that invites expressive oral reading. *Sentences are constructed in a way that underscores and enhances meaning. *Sentences vary in length as well as structure. Fragments, if used, add style. Dialogue, if present, sounds natural. *Purposeful and varied sentence beginnings add variety and energy. *The use of creative and appropriate connectives between sentences and thoughts shows how each relates to and builds upon the one before it. *The writing has cadence; the writer has thought about the sound of the words as well as the meaning. The first time you read it aloud is a breeze.

Comments: _____

Name: _____ Date: _____

Unit 4: Student Writing Rubric—Sentence Fluency

Topic: _____

Type of Writing: *Expository*   *Persuasive*   *Narrative*

Directions: Check those statements that apply to your piece of writing.

_____   My sentences are clear and varied.

_____   My paper has "rhythm" when read aloud; my writing is smooth.

_____   I have used different sentence beginnings; all of my sentences do not begin the same way.

_____   I have written some long sentences and some short sentences.

_____   Some of my sentences are simple, and some are complex.

_____   I used time clues when appropriate.

_____   Every sentence in my paper **is** a sentence; there are no run-on sentences or fragments.

_____   Every sentence is important to the meaning of my paper; there are no unnecessary sentences.

_____   My sentences are concise, not wordy.

_____   My writing is easy for the reader to follow.

Comments: _____

_____

_____

_____

_____

_____

_____

Name: _____ Date: _____

Unit 4: Fluency

Key Ideas
- One characteristic of good writing is **fluency**; that is, writing should have rhythm and smoothness when read aloud.

- **Fluency** means the paper reads well aloud.

- To create **fluency** in writing, sentences should be:
  - varied in length;
  - varied in complexity;
  - concise, not wordy;
  - varied in beginnings; and
  - important to the meaning of the paper.

Practice

Directions: Read each pair of sentences aloud. Decide which of the two has more fluency. Put a ✔ on the line before the number to indicate your choice.

1. _____ a. My father is an authority on stamp collecting.

   _____ b. My father is an authority about stamp collecting.

2. _____ a. Tracy cannot help talking about her new boyfriend to everyone she meets.

   _____ b. Tracy cannot help but to talk about her new boyfriend to everyone she meets.

3. _____ a. The teachers were talking among themselves about the school violence.

   _____ b. The teachers were talking among one another about the school violence.

4. _____ a. Monica graduated high school with top honors.

   _____ b. Monica graduated from high school with top honors.

5. _____ a. According with the book of rules, this should be a corner kick.

   _____ b. According to the book of rules, this should be a corner kick.

On Your Own: Here are some more idiomatic expressions that are often misused. Do you know what the correct phrase should be?

- desirous to
- in search for
- prefer something over something else
- anywheres

Name: _____ Date: _____

Unit 4: Fluency Problems 1

Key Ideas

- One characteristic of good writing is **fluency**; that is, writing should have rhythm and smoothness when read aloud.

- **Fluency** means that the paper reads well aloud.

- To create **fluency** in writing, sentences should be:
  - varied in length;
  - varied in complexity;
  - concise, not wordy;
  - varied in beginnings; and
  - important to the meaning of the paper.

Practice

Directions: Double negatives impede the fluency of a sentence and also convey a meaning the author doesn't intend. (Using two negatives really equals a positive.) Read each of the sentences below, and identify the double negative. Rewrite the sentence correctly on the line below it.

1. Fatima did not see nobody when she entered the ballroom.

   _____

   _____

2. "Don't give me none of your back talk," the policeman said to the gangster.

   _____

   _____

3. After the prom, Katy did not want nothing to do with her date.

   _____

   _____

4. "The thief should not get no respect from the victim," the judge said.

   _____

   _____

5. Frances will not do none of her housework despite her mother's requests.

   _____

   _____

On Your Own: Listen for double negatives in daily conversation, on television, and in radio talk. Try to find some examples to share with your class.

Name: _____ Date: _____

Unit 4: Fluency Problems 2

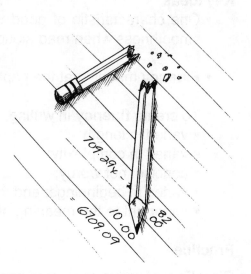

Key Ideas

- One characteristic of good writing is **fluency**; that is, writing should have rhythm and smoothness when read aloud.

- **Fluency** means the paper reads well aloud.

- To create **fluency** in writing, sentences should be:
  - varied in length;
  - varied in complexity;
  - concise, not wordy;
  - varied in beginnings; and
  - important to the meaning of the paper.

Practice

Directions: The following sentences may have fluency problems. Read each one and decide which, if any, of the characteristics above has been violated. Write the characteristic on the line below each sentence.

1. I'm going shopping. You're not coming with me. I am going alone. I want to shop.

   _____

2. I want to be happy and I want to be beautiful and I want to be rich and I want to be famous.

   _____

3. Everyone called me chicken before I kissed her but I was really scared because I had never kissed a girl before and what if she didn't like it or tried to hit me or something?

   _____

4. The boy walked his dog in the park. The boy then did his homework. The boy ate dinner, and then the boy went to bed.

   _____

5. Good grief! My pencil broke right in the middle of the test. Now what would I do?

   _____

Name: _____ Date: _____

Unit 4: Narrative Writing: A Thousand Years From Now

Key Ideas

- A **narrative** is a series of events told like a story; an account of incidents or events written in story form.

- A **narrative** has the following characteristics:

  - **Title** – hints at what the subject of the narrative is about and tries to attract the reader's attention.
  - **Introduction** – contains the topic of the narrative written in an interesting, informative way in order to "grab" the reader's attention and the thesis statement, which expresses the main idea of the narrative.
  - **Body** – develops the thesis statement with examples, facts, incidents, details, and reasons written in an organized, logical way.
  - **Conclusion** – ends the story with a summary of the thesis statement and the writer's thoughts.

Practice

Directions: Make a list of things in your world that you think might not exist in a thousand years from now (the year 3000). Choose the one most interesting to you.

1. Identify it and describe it.

   _____

   _____

   _____

2. Make notes explaining its use and/or importance.

   _____

   _____

   _____

   _____

3. How does this item symbolize our society? In what ways?

   _____

   _____

   _____

   _____

Name: _____　Date: _____

Unit 4: Narrative Writing: A Thousand Years From Now (cont.)

4.　Draft your introductory paragraph here. Remember to include a good, strong thesis statement and to "grab" your reader's attention.

_____

_____

_____

_____

5.　The body of your narrative should include the notes you've written in #2 and #3 above. Organize the information and rewrite as paragraphs. Use your own paper if you need more room.

_____

_____

_____

_____

_____

_____

_____

_____

_____

_____

6.　The ending of your narrative should summarize your main point (can use the information in #1 and #2 above) and draw conclusions or restate your thoughts on the matter.

_____

_____

_____

7.　Think of a couple of good titles for your narrative. Share with a friend. Circle the one you like best.

_____

_____

8.　Rewrite, revise, edit, and polish your narrative for publication.

Name: _____ Date: _____

Unit 4: Writing Skills Test

Directions: Darken the circle next to the choice that is the <u>best</u> answer.

1. Word choice is important in writing because
    - ○ A. selecting the right word helps to communicate meaning.
    - ○ B. it makes the paper more interesting.
    - ○ C. it helps the reader to organize the paper.
    - ○ D. it is important for choosing the right format for the audience.

2. Which one of these <u>best</u> represents what careful word choice can do?
    - ○ A. Help the reader understand the writer's message
    - ○ B. Help the writer communicate the message
    - ○ C. Help the writer clarify and expand his/her ideas
    - ○ D. All of the above

3. Another description of word choice is
    - ○ A. using words that show action, energy, and movement.
    - ○ B. using words that show a good vocabulary.
    - ○ C. using words that the writer looked up in a thesaurus.
    - ○ D. using words that the reader probably won't know.

4. Fluency in writing means
    - ○ A. the writer chose just the right words to make sense.
    - ○ B. the writer chose words that rhyme with each other.
    - ○ C. the writer's words have a rhythm and flow to them.
    - ○ D. the writer's sentences are strong and clear.

5. Fluency can be checked by
    - ○ A. counting the number of three-syllable words.
    - ○ B. looking for the sense of the words.
    - ○ C. checking for irregular word patterns.
    - ○ D. listening for the flow and rhythm when read aloud.

6. Which of the following <u>best</u> describes *figurative language*?
    - ○ A. It is language used in a non-literal way.
    - ○ B. It is language used to write a story.
    - ○ C. It is language used to create vivid mental images.
    - ○ D. It is language used concretely.

7. Which of the following <u>best</u> describes a *narrative*?
    - ○ A. It is a story built on the memory of the writer.
    - ○ B. It is a story recording the writer's private thoughts and ideas.
    - ○ C. It is a series of events or incidents told in story form.
    - ○ D. It is a true story about something that happened to the author.

Name: _____ Date: _____

Unit 4: Writing Skills Test (cont.)

8. Which of the following <u>best</u> describes a *personal narrative*?
    - O A. It is a story built on the memory of the writer.
    - O B. It is a story recording the writer's private thoughts and ideas.
    - O C. It is a series of events or incidents told in story form.
    - O D. It is a true story about something that happened to the author.

9. Which of the following <u>best</u> describes a *narrative journal*?
    - O A. It is a story built on the memory of the writer.
    - O B. It is a story recording the writer's private thoughts and ideas.
    - O C. It is a series of events or incidents told in story form.
    - O D. It is a true story about something that happened to the author.

10. Which of the following <u>best</u> describes a *memoir*?
    - O A. It is a story built on the memory of the writer.
    - O B. It is a story recording the writer's private thoughts and ideas.
    - O C. It is a history of the writer's life.
    - O D. It is a true story about something that happened to the author.

11. Which of the following <u>best</u> describes an *autobiography*?
    - O A. It is a story built on the memory of the writer.
    - O B. It is a story recording the writer's private thoughts and ideas.
    - O C. It is a history of the writer's life.
    - O D. It is a true story about something that happened to the author.

12. Which of the following <u>best</u> describes a *historical narrative*?
    - O A. It is a story built on the memory of the writer.
    - O B. It is a history of the writer's life.
    - O C. It is a story about a significant event in history.
    - O D. It is a true story about something that happened to the author.

13. Which of the following can impede the fluency of a piece of writing?
    - O A. Varied sentence lengths
    - O B. Double negatives
    - O C. Concise sentences
    - O D. Varied sentence complexity

14. Which of the following sentences is the <u>best</u> example of *fluency* in writing?
    - O A. Hungry dog bites trash man.
    - O B. If you teach me the computer, I'll trade in my radio and my stereo and my TV and my little brother.
    - O C. I don't want to go to no summer camp because I hate the outdoors.
    - O D. I fell and hurt my knee, my neck, my head, my back, and my pride.

Name: _____ Date: _____

Unit 4: Writing Skills Test (cont.)

15. Three of the sentences below contain wordy phrases. Which one does <u>not</u>?
    ○ A. Our country is on alert at all times because of potential terrorist attacks.
    ○ B. Our country is always on alert because of potential terrorist attacks.
    ○ C. Our country at the present time is on alert because of potential terrorist attacks.
    ○ D. Due to the fact of terrorist attacks, our country is on alert at all times.

16. Which of the following <u>best</u> represents a *thesis statement*?
    ○ A. This story is about Barbara Baxton and her blue calculator.
    ○ B. Ten-year-old Barbara Baxton loved to compute.
    ○ C. Barbara Baxton got a blue calculator for Christmas.
    ○ D. I am going to tell you about my friend Barbara Baxton.

17. Which one of the following sentences contains a *metaphor*?
    ○ A. The shapes in the dark room looked like monsters to the frightened toddler.
    ○ B. There aren't no children in this house.
    ○ C. My grandfather was a giant among men.
    ○ D. Sammy has two dogs and two cats.

18. Which one of the following sentences contains a *simile*?
    ○ A. The shapes in the dark room looked like monsters to the frightened toddler.
    ○ B. There aren't no children in this house.
    ○ C. My grandfather was a giant among men.
    ○ D. Sammy has two dogs and two cats.

19. Which one of the following sentences contains a *double negative*?
    ○ A. The shapes in the dark room looked like monsters to the frightened toddler.
    ○ B. There aren't no children in this house.
    ○ C. My grandfather was a giant among men.
    ○ D. Sammy has two dogs and two cats.

Name: _____ Date: _____

Unit 4: Writing Skills Test (cont.)

20.–25.   Writing Sample: **What Freedom Means to Me**

- Write a narrative that informs readers about your definition of freedom. Be sure to include reasons, examples, facts, details, and/or incidents that support your definition.

- Before you begin writing, use scratch paper to organize your ideas. Organization is important, as is following the characteristics for a good narrative: title, introductory paragraph, body, and concluding or summarizing paragraph.

- Use the best English you can, but do not worry about mistakes. The most important things are word choice and fluency; they will be the emphasis of evaluation for this writing sample.

_____

_____

_____

_____

_____

_____

_____

_____

_____

_____

_____

_____

_____

_____

Section II: Conventions of Writing

The Importance of Conventions

★ Conventions are the mechanical correctness of the piece—spelling, grammar and usage, paragraphing, capitalization, and punctuation.

★ Writing with strong conventions has been proofread and edited with care.

★ Writing with strong conventions needs little editing to prepare it for publication.

★ Sophistication in use of conventions should increase as students get older.

★ Conventions may be manipulated for stylistic effect.

Name: _____ Date: _____

Topic: _____

Type of Writing: _____

6. Scoring Rubric for Evaluating Conventions

Directions: Circle the number that best describes the quality of the writing.

1 Not Yet: A bare beginning; writer not yet showing any control
2 Emerging: Need for revision outweighs strengths; isolated moments hint at what the writer has in mind
3 Developing: Strengths and need for revision are about equal; about halfway home
4 Effective: On balance, the strengths outweigh the weaknesses; a small amount of revision is needed
5 Strong: Shows control and skill in this trait; many strengths present
6 Wow! Exceeds expectations

Features	Not Yet	Emerging	Developing	Effective	Strong
Conventions:	**1**	**2**	**3**	**4**	**5**
	Errors in spelling, punctuation, capitalization, usage, grammar, and/or paragraphing repeatedly distract the reader and make the text difficult to read. The writing reflects more than one of these problems: *Spelling errors are frequent, even on common words. *Punctuation (including terminal punctuation) is often missing or incorrect. *Capitalization is random, and only the easiest rules show awareness of correct use. *Errors in grammar or usage are very noticeable and frequent and affect meaning. *Paragraphing is missing, irregular, or so frequent (every sentence) that it has no relationship to the organizational structure of the text. *The reader must read once to decode, then again for meaning. Extensive editing (virtually every line) would be required to polish the text for publication.		The writer shows reasonable control over a limited range of standard writing conventions. Conventions are sometimes handled well and enhance readability; at other times, errors are distracting and impair readability. *Spelling is usually correct or reasonably phonetic on common words, but more difficult words are problematic. *End punctuation is usually correct; internal punctuation (*commas, apostrophes, semicolons, dashes, colons, parentheses*) is sometimes missing/wrong. *Most words are capitalized correctly; control over more sophisticated capitalization skills may be spotty. *Problems with grammar or usage are not serious enough to distort meaning but may not be correct or accurately applied all of the time. *Paragraphing is attempted but may run together or begin in the wrong places. *Moderate editing (a little of this, a little of that) would be required to polish the text for publication.		The writer demonstrates a good grasp of standard writing conventions (spelling, punctuation, capitalization, grammar, usage, paragraphing) and uses conventions effectively to enhance readability. Errors tend to be so few that just minor touchups would get this piece ready to publish. *Spelling is generally correct, even on more difficult words. *The punctuation is accurate, even creative, and guides the reader through the text. *A thorough understanding and consistent application of capitalization skills are present. *Grammar and usage are correct and contribute to clarity and style. *Paragraphing tends to be sound and reinforces the organizational structure. *The writer may manipulate conventions for stylistic effect—and it works! The piece is very close to being ready to publish. *Writing shows control over those conventions that are grade/age appropriate.

Comments: _____

Used with permission from the Northwest Regional Educational Laboratory (NWREL).

Section II: Conventions of Writing

The Importance of Presentation

★ Presentation is the way a writer exhibits a message on paper, the way the writing looks on the page.

★ The paper is inviting to read when the guidelines for good presentation are observed.

★ Presentation has to do with how the paper looks: the handwriting, the margins, the neatness, and the general, overall appearance.

★ Good writers are aware of the necessity of presentation. If graphics, maps, charts, and graphs are included, they should be appropriate and help guide the reader through the text.

★ A writer is concerned about presentation during the publication stage of the writing process.

Used with permission from the Northwest Regional Educational Laboratory (NWREL).

Name: _____ Date: _____

Topic: _____

Type of Writing: _____

Plus 1 - Scoring Rubric for Evaluating Presentation

Directions: Circle the number that best describes the quality of the writing.

1 **Not Yet:**   A bare beginning; writer not yet showing any control
2 **Emerging:**   Need for revision outweighs strengths; isolated moments hint at what the writer has in mind
3 **Developing:**   Strengths and need for revision are about equal; about halfway home
4 **Effective:**   On balance, the strengths outweigh the weaknesses; a small amount of revision is needed
5 **Strong:**   Shows control and skill in this trait; many strengths present
6 **Wow!**   Exceeds expectations

Features	Not Yet	Emerging	Developing	Effective	Strong
Presentation:	1	2	3	4	5
	The reader receives a garbled message due to problems relating to the presentation of the text. *Because the letters are irregularly slanted, formed inconsistently or incorrectly, and the spacing is unbalanced or not even present, it is very difficult to read and understand the text. *The writer has gone wild with multiple fonts and font sizes. It is a major distraction to the reader. *The spacing is random and confusing to the reader. There may be little or no white space on the page. *Lack of markers (title, page numbering, bullets, side heads/subheads, etc.) leaves the reader wondering how one section connects to another and why the text is organized in this manner on the page. *The visuals do not support or further illustrate key ideas presented in the text. They may be misleading, indecipherable, or too complex to be understood.	**The writer's message is understandable in this format.** *Handwriting is readable, although there may be discrepancies in letter shape and form, slant, and spacing that may make some words or passages easier to read than others. *Experimentation with fonts and font sizes is successful in some places, but begins to get fussy and cluttered in others. The effect is not consistent throughout the text. *While margins may be present, some text may crowd the edges. Consistent spacing is applied, although a different choice may make text more accessible (for example: single, double, or triple spacing). *Although some markers are present (titles, numbering, bullets, side heads/subheads, etc.), they are not used to their fullest potential as a guide for the reader to access the greatest meaning from the text. *An attempt is made to integrate visuals and the text, although the connections may be limited.		**The form and presentation of the text enhance the reader's ability to understand and connect with the message. It is pleasing to the eye.** * If handwritten, slant is consistent, letters are clearly formed, spacing is uniform, and text is easy to read. * If word-processed, there is appropriate use of fonts and font sizes, which invites the reader into the text. *The use of white space on the page (spacing, margins, etc.) allows the reader to focus on the text and message without distractions. There is balance between white space and text on the page. The formatting suits the purpose for writing. * A title, side heads/subheads, page numbers, bullets, and evidence of correct use of a style sheet (when appropriate) make the hierarchy of information clear to the reader. * If appropriate to the audience and purpose, there is effective integration of charts, graphs, maps, illustrations, etc. There is clear alignment between text and visuals. The visuals support and clarify important information or key points.

Comments: _____

Used with permission from the Northwest Regional Educational Laboratory (NWREL).

Name: _____ Date: _____

Section II: Student Writing Rubric—Conventions/Presentation

Topic: _____

Type of Writing: *Expository*   *Persuasive*   *Narrative*

Directions: Check those statements that apply to your writing.

_____   My spelling is correct.

_____   My punctuation is correct.

_____   My grammar is correct.

_____   I carefully revised this paper.

_____   I carefully edited this paper.

_____   There are no significant errors in my paper.

_____   My format is appropriate to my audience and for my purpose.

_____   I followed the format given with the assignment.

_____   My paper has a pleasing layout and effective use of white space.

_____   Readers can read my handwriting.

_____   I have a "dy-no-mite" title for my paper.

Comments: _____

_____

_____

_____

_____

_____

Name: _____ Date: _____

Section II: Conventions of Writing

Key Ideas

- **Conventions** are the mechanics of writing: spelling, grammar, usage, paragraphing, capitalization, and punctuation.

- Writing that is strong in **conventions** has been carefully proofed and edited to eliminate these types of errors.

Practice

Directions: Read the following paragraph carefully. Proof any errors using the editor's marks listed below. There are 22 errors in conventions—can you find them all? Write the corrections on the lines below.

No More circus!

For my brithday, mom and dad said I could redecorate my bedroom. The last time it was decroated was when I was for yearsold. Its time to say good-bye to the circis theme—no more big top canapy, elephants, lions, tiggers, or clowns. My new wallpaper and bedspread will have Race cars Monster trucks and Motorcycles on them. My parents' are even going to by me a computerdesk and a computer, so I can do my homework in my room ill have the coolest bedroom ever!

sp.	Spelling
☰	Capitalize
/	Make lower case
ᶹ	Insert apostrophe
⚹	Insert space
⌃	Insert comma
⊙	Insert period
¶	New paragraph
⤳	Delete word

---

1. _____ 2. _____

3. _____ 4. _____

5. _____ 6. _____

7. _____ 8. _____

9. _____ 10. _____

11. _____ 12. _____

13. _____ 14. _____

15. _____ 16. _____

17. _____ 18. _____

19. _____ 20. _____

21. _____ 22. _____

Name: _____ Date: _____

Unit 5: Punctuation: Commas 1

Key Ideas

- In general, a **comma** is used to separate words or phrases to make their meanings more clear.

- A **comma** is used to separate introductory words, phrases, and clauses.
  Example: Slowly, she turned and walked toward the door.

- A **comma** is used to separate words in a series or a list.
  Example: I hurt my elbow, my knee, and my ankle when I fell off my bike.

  (Do not use a comma before the first word in a list or after the last word in a list.)

- **Commas** are used to separate phrases in a series.
  Example: Tom won three gold medals, two silver medals, and one bronze medal in the Olympics.

Practice

Directions: In the following sentences, insert commas where necessary to separate words or phrases, using the editor's mark (⩔) .

1. He has plundered our seas ravaged our coasts burnt our towns and destroyed the lives of

   our people.   —*Declaration of Independence*

2. The long twisting muddy road led to the private cabin in the woods.

3. To win a gold medal Bonnie needed a lot of luck.

4. When I opened the junk drawer the scissors tape ruler and stapler fell out.

5. At the video arcade Jason lost all of his allowance his jacket and his package.

6. To make hot chocolate heat the milk slowly stirring constantly and then add the mix.

7. For dinner we had a choice of steak chicken or seafood.

8. When in doubt ask someone for advice.

85

Unit 5: Punctuation: Commas 2

Key Ideas

- In general, a **comma** is used to separate words or phrases to make their meanings more clear.

- A **comma** is used to enclose a word or phrase that follows a noun and describes it. This is called an **appositive**.
  Example: We visited Aunt Mary, my mother's sister, yesterday.

- A **comma** is used to separate two adjectives modifying the same noun.
  Example: This supermarket has the most ripe, delicious fruit.

- A **comma** is used before (or after) a quotation, as in dialogue.
  Example 1:   My brother yelled, "I'll race you home."
  Example 2:   "Okay," I hollered back.

Practice

Directions: Using the editor's mark(⌃), insert commas in the following paragraph where they are needed.

> Last week I saw my friend Randy in the bookstore. She was sitting in a chair with three books two magazines and four pens. "Yo" I said. When she saw me she winked smiled and said "Hi!" I asked her if she was waiting for her mother Helen to come pick her up. Nodding her head she said that she had been waiting here at the photo mart and at the doctor's for her mom to finish her shopping her yoga lesson and her errands. "Once she finishes" she said "I'll get to go home!"

On Your Own: When writing, edit for commas carefully. Check every sentence that doesn't begin with the subject to see whether it opens with an introductory word, phrase, or clause that tells when, where, how, or why the main action of the sentence occurs. If so, make sure you've separated the introduction from the main part of the sentence with a comma.

Name: _____ Date: _____

Unit 5: Punctuation: Dashes

Key Ideas
- **Dashes** set off ideas that are separate from the main sentence.
  Example: Aunt Joann—a wild and wacky woman—is my mother's older sister.

- **Dashes** are similar to commas but emphasize a description or thought more emphatically.
  Example: The St. Louis Rams—my favorite team—may win the Super Bowl.

- **Dashes** may also be used to introduce a word or group of words more forcefully.
  Example: Barb needs only one thing to make her day complete—a pizza.

Practice

Directions: Rewrite the following sentences on the lines below, inserting dashes where needed.

1. Katie knows how to cook three things spaghetti, egg sandwiches, and macaroni and cheese.

   _____

   _____

2. Robbie my all-time favorite friend was absent today.

   _____

   _____

3. Are you sure you have the right phone number 555-2718?

   _____

   _____

4. The person I least wanted to see showed up at the dance Grant Fowler.

   _____

   _____

5. Bob Marley a really annoying person sits behind me in social studies.

   _____

   _____

On Your Own: Use dashes carefully and sparingly. They are somewhat informal but can also cause a break in the rhythm and flow in reading. Too many of them create a jerky, disconnected effect that makes it hard for the reader to follow your thoughts.

Name: _____ Date: _____

Unit 5: Punctuation: Parentheses

Key Ideas

- Use **parentheses** to enclose material or ideas that are of minor importance in the sentence.

    Example: Kearney Scott was elected (once again) as class president.

- Use **parentheses** around the abbreviation of an organization after its full name.

    Example: My Uncle Sam works for the National Aeronautics and Space Administration (NASA).

- Use **parentheses** to enclose numbers or letters in a list.

    Example: Mom wants five things from the market: (1) eggs, (2) milk, (3) bread, (4) rice, and (5) yeast.

Practice

Directions: Insert parentheses where they belong in the following sentences:

1. Our topics today are a election of officers, b forming committees, and c setting the date for the next dance.

2. David Hamilton you met him last Sunday will be at the wedding reception.

3. Do you know where the Society for the Prevention of Cruelty to Animals SPCA is located?

4. This map I am sure it is accurate should lead us to the treasure.

5. Marysia she is my cousin from Croatia is coming for a visit this summer.

6. You can call our family 800 number 1-800-555-6566 to reach me anytime.

7. Turn to Chapter 3 in your book pages 73–91.

8. In social studies, we read about the Klu Klux Klan's KKK activity during the pre-civil rights era.

Write a sentence that includes parentheses on the lines below.

_____

_____

Name: _____ Date: _____

Unit 5: Punctuation: End Punctuation

Key Ideas

- A **period**, a **question mark**, and an **exclamation** point are like STOP signs on a road. They signal the reader to come to a complete stop.

- A **period** marks the end of a sentence that makes a statement (a declarative sentence) or gives a command (an imperative sentence).
    Examples: Vashti is moving to Arkansas.
    The Menard family is having a garage sale.
    Shut the door quietly.

- A **question mark** ends a sentence that asks a question (an interrogative sentence).
    Examples: Where are your mom and dad?
    Does Vanessa like her after-school job?

- An **exclamation point** ends a sentence that expresses strong feelings or forceful commands (an exclamatory or imperative sentence).
    Examples: What a great teacher you are!
    Hurry up, and get out of the cold!

Practice

Directions: Insert the correct punctuation mark at the end of each of the following sentences.

1. What a cute little boy

2. What grade are you in now

3. Gary will be in cub scouts next year

4. Look what time it is

5. What time is your mother picking you up

6. I have to work one more hour before the dinner break

7. You boys stop fighting

8. Did you wash your hands

9. The pool will be open throughout our vacation.

10. Ow, that hurts

89

Name: _____ Date: _____

Unit 5: Punctuation: Semicolons 1

Key Ideas

- A **semicolon** is stronger than a comma but not as strong as a period in telling the reader what to do.

- Use a **semicolon** to separate independent clauses (clauses that have a subject and a predicate) not joined by a conjunction.
  Examples: My science class is third period; math class is last period.

* **Note:** Each clause, *my science class is third period,* and *math class is last period,* could stand alone as a sentence because each has a subject and a predicate. That is why they are called **independent clauses**.

Practice

Directions: Check the sentence that is correctly punctuated in each group below.

1. ❑ a.   I had three raffle tickets left, Uncle Bob bought two of them.
   ❑ b.   I had three raffle tickets left; Uncle Bob bought two of them.

2. ❑ a.   Sammy wants to go to the movies, and so does Susan.
   ❑ b.   Sammy wants to go to the movies; and so does Susan.

3. ❑ a.   Every kid should have access to a computer, Internet service should be free.
   ❑ b.   Every kid should have access to a computer; Internet service should be free.

4. ❑ a.   Robert Fulton trained as an artist, but he invented a successful steamboat.
   ❑ b.   Robert Fulton trained as an artist; but he invented a successful steamboat.

5. ❑ a.   When I am twenty-one, I will get my own apartment.
   ❑ b.   When I am twenty-one; I will get my own apartment.

6. ❑ a.   Agnes is hungry, she wants a pizza.
   ❑ b.   Agnes is hungry; she wants a pizza.

On Your Own: Write two sentences that contain independent clauses not joined by a conjunction. Do not punctuate them. Give them to a partner and have him/her punctuate your sentences correctly.

Name: _____ Date: _____

Unit 5: Punctuation: Semicolons 2

Key Ideas

- A **semicolon** is stronger than a comma but not as strong as a period in telling the reader what to do.

- Use a **semicolon** to separate independent clauses if they are joined by adverbs, such as *however, also, besides, indeed, in fact, otherwise, furthermore,* etc.
  Example: We want to come to your party; however, Mary has a bad cold.

Practice

Directions: Check the sentence in each group that is correctly punctuated.

1. ❑ a.   Barry is ready, however, his date is not.
   ❑ b.   Barry is ready; however, his date is not.

2. ❑ a.   Mr. Hickman is not a nice person, and he has a bad temper.
   ❑ b.   Mr. Hickman is not a nice person; and, he has a bad temper.

3. ❑ a.   Katie does not like chocolate, besides, she is allergic to it.
   ❑ b.   Katie does not like chocolate; besides, she is allergic to it.

4. ❑ a.   My baby sister loves yogurt, her favorite flavor is lemon.
   ❑ b.   My baby sister loves yogurt; her favorite flavor is lemon.

5. ❑ a.   I like Girl Scout Cookies, in fact, I could eat a whole box of them.
   ❑ b.   I like Girl Scout Cookies; in fact, I could eat a whole box of them.

6. ❑ a.   It is a long ride to Nana's house, therefore, I will take a book and some CDs.
   ❑ b.   It is a long ride to Nana's house; therefore, I will take a book and some CDs.

7. ❑ a.   The police found fingerprints on the table, which they used to identify the thief.
   ❑ b.   The police found fingerprints on the table; which they used to identify the thief.

8. ❑ a.   Donnie wrote two term papers, moreover, he also did the project.
   ❑ b.   Donnie wrote two term papers; moreover, he also did the project.

On Your Own: Write two sentences that contain independent clauses that are joined by one of the adverbs listed above. Do not punctuate them. Give your sentences to a partner and have him/her punctuate your sentences correctly. Check your partner's work.

91

Name: _____ Date: _____

Unit 5: Punctuation: Semicolons 3

Key Ideas

- A **semicolon** is stronger than a comma but not as strong as a period in telling the reader what to do.

- Use a **semicolon** to separate a series of things when commas are used as part of the things.
    Example: Aunt Ida has three pets: Hobbs, the cat; Bubba, the dog; and Barnaby, the goat.

Practice

Directions: Check the correctly punctuated sentence in each group.

1. ❑ a.   Mr. Smith, the vice-president; Ms. Nichols, the president; and Mrs. Boyett, the secretary, will all attend the meeting.
   ❑ b.   Mr. Smith, the vice-president, Ms. Nichols, the president, and Mrs. Boyett, the secretary, will all attend the meeting.

2. ❑ a.   Theo, my brother; Derrick, my cousin; and Kerry, my friend, are all coming to the party.
   ❑ b.   Theo, my brother, Derrick, my cousin, and Kerry, my friend, are all coming to the party.

3. ❑ a.   Advanced algebra is hard, however, I like the class.
   ❑ b.   Advanced algebra is hard; however, I like the class.

4. ❑ a.   She likes three types of music: pop, like N'Sync; blues, like Miles Davis; and rap, like Nelly.
   ❑ b.   She likes three types of music: pop, like N'Sync, blues, like Miles Davis, and rap, like Nelly.

5. ❑ a.   Our class surveyed 150 students; more than two-thirds of them watch MTV.
   ❑ b.   Our class surveyed 150 students, more than two-thirds of them watch MTV.

6. ❑ a.   It was snowing hard; otherwise, I would have been home on time.
   ❑ b.   It was snowing hard, otherwise I would have been home on time.

On Your Own: Write two sentences that contain a list of items that includes commas. Do not punctuate the sentences. Give them to a partner and have him/her punctuate your sentences correctly. Check your partner's work.

Name: _____ Date: _____

Unit 5: Punctuation: Apostrophes 1

Key Ideas

- The **apostrophe** has two meanings. It either shows possession or that something has been left out.

  - The **apostrophe** shows ownership (possession) by someone or something.
    Example 1:　　Momar's dog is running loose through the neighborhood.
    (The apostrophe signals the reader that the *dog* belongs to Momar.)

    Example 2:　　The children's book section was crowded with kids.
    (The apostrophe signals the reader that the *book section* belongs to the children.)

  - When the noun is plural, the **apostrophe** goes after the *s* in the word.
    Example 3:　　The students' books are on the teachers' desks.
    (The apostrophes signal the reader that the *books* belong to the students and the *desks* belong to the teachers.)

    Example 4:　　The wolves' howling made it hard to get to sleep.
    (The apostrophe signals the reader that the *howling* belongs to the wolves.)

  - Do not use an **apostrophe** with personal possessive pronouns: *my, mine, your, yours, his, her, hers, its, our, your, yours, their, theirs.* These possessive pronouns already show possession.
    Example 5:　　Victoria left **her** violin in the vestibule.
    (The possessive pronoun *her* signals the reader that the *violin* belongs to Victoria.)

    Example 6:　　The lion only obeys **its** trainer.
    (The possessive pronoun *its* signals the reader that the *trainer* belongs to the lion.)

Practice

Directions: Complete the following sentences by inserting the correct word.

1. The gardener took very good care of the _____ roses. (The roses belong to the queen.)

2. Martin came home to a _____ welcome. (The welcome belongs to the hero.)

3. The dog chewed right through _____ collar. (The collar belongs to the dog.)

4. The door to the _____ locker room stood ajar. (The locker room belongs to the ladies.)

Name: _____ Date: _____

Unit 5: Punctuation: Apostrophes 1 (cont.)

5. Is this computer _____? (The computer belongs to you.)

6. The _____ veil got caught in the door. (The veil belongs to the bride.)

7. This barn is where we keep the _____ bridles. (The bridles belong to the horses.)

8. That spelling paper is _____. (The paper belongs to me.)

9. _____ soccer team is the best in our division. (The team belongs to Phil.)

10. My _____ dry cleaners is in this shopping mall. (The dry cleaners belongs to the parents.)

Directions: Write the sentences on the lines below, adding apostrophes where needed.

1. Malcolms dog is wagging its tail.

    _____

2. Zanes sister is the star player on the girls basketball team.

    _____

    _____

3. I do not always agree with my teachers interpretations of the stories we read.

    _____

    _____

4. Sarahs mother called the school and said that she was sick today.

    _____

    _____

5. Your hamsters food is in its dish on the teachers desk.

    _____

    _____

On Your Own: Write one sentence that contains apostrophes showing possession for the following words: *lock, Jess, girl.* Use all three words in one sentence.

Name: _____ Date: _____

Unit 5: Punctuation: Apostrophes 2

Key Ideas

- The **apostrophe** has two meanings. It either shows possession or that something has been left out.

  - The **apostrophe** shows ownership (possession) by someone or something.
    Example: Ming's prom dress is beautiful.
    (The apostrophe signals the reader that the prom dress belongs to Ming.)

  - The **apostrophe** is used to show that something (a letter or number) has been left out.
    Example 1:   I really don't want to miss that movie.
    (*Don't* means *do not.* The *o* in *not* is left out. The apostrophe takes its place.)

    Example 2:   I graduated in the class of '99.
    (*'99* means *1999.* The apostrophe took the place of the digits *19.*)

Practice

Directions: Correct the following sentences by inserting apostrophes where needed.

1. Isnt it a beautiful day?

2. Theyre on the teachers desk behind her calendar.

3. Nicholass shoes are always in the middle of the floor.

4. Arent the childrens stories this year better than last years

   stories?

5. Were studying South Americas geography and Brazils language, Portuguese.

6. It doesnt look like rain for todays baseball game.

7. I just cant do what the coach wants me to do with the teams equipment.

8. Iras car is in my fathers shop waiting for its tune-up.

On Your Own: Be very careful of the frequently confused words *its* and *it's. It's* always stands for *it is;* otherwise, use *its,* which shows possession.

Name: _____ Date: _____

Unit 5: Punctuation Test

Directions: Identify the correctly punctuated sentence in each group by darkening the circle next to the correct sentence.

1. ○ A. When Sarah finishes eating; she'll take a nap.
   ○ B. When Sarah finishes eating: she'll take a nap.
   ○ C. When Sarah finishes eating, she'll take a nap.
   ○ D. When Sarah finishes eating she'll take a nap.

2. ○ A. Where would you like to go tomorrow Rusty?
   ○ B. Where would you like to go tomorrow, Rusty?
   ○ C. Where, would you like to go tomorrow Rusty?
   ○ D. Where would you, like to go tomorrow Rusty?

3. ○ A. Mother wants you to sweep the stairs, wash the floor, and vacuum the rug.
   ○ B. Mother wants you to, sweep the stairs, wash the floor, and vacuum the rug.
   ○ C. Mother wants you to sweep the stairs, wash the floor, and, vacuum the rug.
   ○ D. Mother wants you, to sweep the stairs, wash the floor, and, vacuum the rug.

4. ○ A. Stop Susan's coach wants to talk to you.
   ○ B. Stop! Susan's coach wants to talk to you.
   ○ C. Stop, Susan's coach wants to talk to you.
   ○ D. Stop. Susan's coach wants to talk to you.

5. ○ A. My brother is smart handsome and successful.
   ○ B. My brother, is smart handsome and successful.
   ○ C. My brother is smart, handsome, and successful.
   ○ D. My brother is smart, handsome, and, successful.

6. ○ A. Here, take the posters and hang them in the hallway, the cafeteria, and the office.
   ○ B. Here, take the posters and hang them in the hallway the cafeteria and the office.
   ○ C. Here take the posters, and hang them in the hallway, the cafeteria and the office.
   ○ D. Here take the posters, and hang them, in the hallway, the cafeteria and the office.

7. ○ A. This week I have three finals, two term papers, and an oral exam.
   ○ B. This week: I have three finals; two term papers; and an oral exam.
   ○ C. This week, I have three finals; two term papers; and an oral exam.
   ○ D. This week I have: three finals, two term papers, and an oral exam.

8. ○ A. Coyly she flirted with the cute computer technician.
   ○ B. Coyly, she flirted with the cute, computer technician.
   ○ C. Coyly, she flirted with the cute computer technician.
   ○ D. Coyly; she flirted with the cute computer technician.

Name: _____ Date: _____

Unit 5: Punctuation Test (cont.)

9. ○ A. We are going to Alaska to see my father's brother Andy.
   ○ B. We are going to Alaska to see my fathers brother, Andy.
   ○ C. We are going to Alaska; to see my father's brother Andy.
   ○ D. We are going to Alaska to see my father's brother, Andy.

10. ○ A. She visited Mr. Williamson; her favorite teacher; last night.
    ○ B. She visited Mr. Williamson, her favorite teacher last night.
    ○ C. She visited Mr. Williamson, her favorite teacher, last night.
    ○ D. She visited Mr. Williamson her favorite teacher last night.

11. ○ A. Katie said to her mother, "did you see me score?"
    ○ B. Katie said to her mother "Did you see me score?"
    ○ C. Katie said to her mother, "Did you see me score?"
    ○ D. Katie said, to her mother, "Did you see me score."

12. ○ A. He walked north along Pine Street—a very dangerous road.
    ○ B. He walked north along Pine street, a very dangerous road.
    ○ C. He walked North along Pine Street; a very dangerous road.
    ○ D. He walked north along pine street—a very dangerous road.

13. ○ A. I only need one more thing; a quarter, to complete my collection.
    ○ B. I only need one more thing—a quarter—to complete my collection.
    ○ C. I only need one more thing a quarter to complete my collection.
    ○ D. I only need one more thing, a quarter, to complete my collection.

14. ○ A. Are you sure you have the right address 706 Chicago Dr.?
    ○ B. Are you sure you have the right address, 706 Chicago Dr.?
    ○ C. Are you sure you have the right address—706 Chicago Dr.?
    ○ D. Are you sure, you have the right address—706 Chicago Dr.?

15. ○ A. To get a subscription, just call the 800 number; 1-800-555-TEST.
    ○ B. To get a subscription, just call the 800 number—1-800-555-TEST.
    ○ C. To get a subscription, just call the 800 number 1-800-555-TEST.
    ○ D. To get a subscription, just call the 800 number (1-800-555-TEST).

16. ○ A. What a cute baby.
    ○ B. What a cute baby!
    ○ C. What a cute baby?

17. ○ A. Hold tightly to my hand, Brian.
    ○ B. Hold tightly to my hand, Brian!
    ○ C. Hold tightly to my hand, Brian?

Name: _____ Date: _____

Unit 5: Punctuation Test (cont.)

18. ○ A. Is our check in the mail.
     ○ B. Is our check in the mail!
     ○ C. Is our check in the mail?

19. ○ A. Don't do that.
     ○ B. Don't do that!
     ○ C. Don't do that?

20. ○ A. The gym has extended its hours during the vacation.
     ○ B. The gym has extended its hours during the vacation!
     ○ C. The gym has extended its hours during the vacation?

21. ○ A. You may enter the temple I have to take my shoes off first.
     ○ B. You may enter the temple, I have to take my shoes off first.
     ○ C. You may enter the temple; I have to take my shoes off first.

22. ○ A. We have to leave but Savannah can stay.
     ○ B. We have to leave, but Savannah can stay.
     ○ C. We have to leave; but Savannah can stay.
     ○ D. We have to leave, but, Savannah can stay.

23. ○ A. When Ardith stepped on the plane she started to perspire heavily.
     ○ B. When Ardith stepped on the plane, she started to perspire heavily.
     ○ C. When Ardith stepped on the plane; she started to perspire heavily.
     ○ D. When Ardith stepped on the plane; She started to perspire heavily.

24. ○ A. Nolan bought a brand new car it was a convertible.
     ○ B. Nolan bought a brand new car, it was a convertible.
     ○ C. Nolan bought a brand new car; it was a convertible.
     ○ D. Nolan bought a brand new car; It was a convertible.

25. ○ A. Jamie is home with a cold otherwise she would be at the party.
     ○ B. Jamie is home with a cold, otherwise she would be at the party.
     ○ C. Jamie is home with a cold, otherwise, she would be at the party.
     ○ D. Jamie is home with a cold; otherwise, she would be at the party.

26. ○ A. The doctors nurse called me with the results of the test.
     ○ B. The doctor's nurse called me with the results of the test.

27. ○ A. Sister's week is when the four of us get together.
     ○ B. Sisters' week is when the four of us get together.

Name: _____ Date: _____

Unit 5: Punctuation Test (cont.)

28. ○ A. Wed go to the football game if we had tickets.
    ○ B. We'd go to the football game if we had tickets.

29. ○ A. 92 was a very good year for us.
    ○ B. '92 was a very good year for us.

30. ○ A. The weather person said its going to rain on Wednesday.
    ○ B. The weather person said it's going to rain on Wednesday.

Write two sentences that correctly use an apostrophe.

31. _____

32. _____

Write two sentences that contain commas used in two different ways.

33. _____

34. _____

Write two sentences that correctly use semicolons.

35. _____

36. _____

Write two sentences, one which correctly includes a dash and one which correctly includes the use of parentheses.

37. _____

38. _____

Write four sentences, one a declarative sentence, one an imperative sentence, one an exclamatory sentence, and one an interrogative sentence. Punctuate all correctly.

39. _____

40. _____

41. _____

42. _____

Name: _____ Date: _____

Unit 6: Spelling/Usage: Suffixes *-ant, -ance, -ent,* and *-ence*

Key Idea
- When adding the **suffixes**, *-ant*, *-ance*, *-ent*, and *-ence*, it is often helpful to think of a related word before spelling the suffix.

> *Examples:* significant = significance
> intelligent = intelligence

Practice

Directions: Add the proper suffix (*-ance* or *-ence*) to the root of each of the words below. Think of the related word before spelling the suffix. Use a dictionary if you need help.

1. assistant _____

2. abundant _____

3. excellent _____

4. patient _____

5. obedient _____

6. distant _____

7. different _____

8. repent _____

9. avoid _____

10. succulent _____

11. permanent _____

12. convenient _____

13. elegant _____

14. resistant _____

15. important _____

16. absent _____

17. imminent _____

18. annoy _____

19. violent _____

20. defy _____

On Your Own: Have you figured out that the suffixes *-ant* and *-ent* mean "one who"? These words are adjectives. Have you also figured out that the suffixes *-ance* and *-ence* mean "state or quality of"? These words are nouns.

100

Name: _____ Date: _____

Unit 6: Spelling/Usage: Suffixes -*able* and -*ible*

Key Ideas

- The **suffix** -***able*** is usually added to base words (e.g., base word + suffix = new word).

  Examples: desire   desirable
  rely   reliable
  allow   allowable

- The **suffix** -***ible*** is usually added to word roots (e.g., root + ible = new word).

  Examples: legible   divisible
  audible   gullible

Practice

Directions: Choose and circle the correct spelling of each of the following pairs of words. Be sure to explain why you chose the word you did based on the key ideas above.

1.	eligible	eligable	2.	perishible	perishable
3.	lovible	lovable	4.	impossible	impossable
5.	reliable	reliible	6.	sensible	sensable
7.	eatible	eatable	8.	possible	possable
9.	edible	edable	10.	readible	readable
11.	enjoyible	enjoyable	12.	expressible	expressable
13.	acceptible	acceptable	14.	playible	playable
15.	washible	washable	16.	payible	payable
17.	incredible	incredable	18.	conquerible	conquerable
19.	legible	legable	20.	plausible	plausable

On Your Own: Can you think of two new words that fit this category? Give them to a friend for spelling.

Name: _____ Date: _____

Unit 6: Spelling/Usage: Suffixes *-ology* and *-ologist*

Key Ideas

• The Greek **suffix *-ology*** means "the study of." It is used with other root words.

   Examples: sociology   =   the study of human society

               cardiology   =   the study of the heart

• The Greek **suffix *-ist*** means "one who practices" so that:

   Examples: sociologist   =   one who practices the study of human society

               cardiologist =   one who practices the study of the heart

Practice

Directions: For each of the words below, make an educated guess as to what the word means.

1. Cosmologist _____

2. Musicology _____

3. Zoology _____

4. Geologist _____

5. Hydrology _____

6. Volcanologist _____

7. Radiology _____

8. Paleontologist _____

9. Pharmacology _____

10. Psychologist _____

On Your Own: Can you think of three other words with one of these suffixes? Give them to a friend, and see if he/she can guess the definition.

102

Name: _____ Date: _____

Unit 6: Spelling/Usage: Compound Words

Key Ideas

- **Compound words** do not always retain the meanings of the two words used. The new compound word often has a new meaning not closely related to the original words.

    Examples: brainstorm
    copperhead

- **Compound words** may be spelled as one word, as a hyphenated word, or as two separate words.

    Examples: rainbow
    long-lived
    cold front

Practice

Directions: Combine the two words to make a third word. Define the third word. Use a dictionary if you need help.

1. door   +   knob   =   _____

_____

2. light   +   weight   =   _____

_____

3. long   +   legged   =   _____

_____

4. wire   +   tapping   =   _____

_____

5. man   +   hunt   =   _____

_____

6. news   +   stand   =   _____

_____

Unit 6: Spelling/Usage: Borrowed Words

Key Ideas

- Words from many other languages have become part of the English language. Here are some of the more common **borrowed words**:

mosquito	guitar	karate	jungle
pajamas	shampoo	souvenir	casserole
tomato	chocolate	rodeo	patio
camouflage	ketchup	chipmunk	bagel
vanilla	tulip	zebra	knapsack

- For a **borrowed word** to become part of the English language, it must become popular with English speakers and have a definition that everyone agrees on.

Practice

Directions: Use a dictionary to write the meaning of each word below and the language from which it came on the line next to the word.

1. mosquito _____

2. guitar _____

3. karate _____

4. jungle _____

5. pajamas _____

6. shampoo _____

7. souvenir _____

8. casserole _____

9. tomato _____

10. chocolate _____

11. rodeo _____

12. patio _____

13. camouflage _____

Name: _____ Date: _____

Unit 6: Spelling/Usage: Borrowed Words (cont.)

14. ketchup _____

15. chipmunk _____

16. bagel _____

17. vanilla _____

18. tulip _____

19. zebra _____

20. knapsack _____

Directions: Can you find three to five more words that are originally from another language and have become some of our "borrowed" words? Be sure to include the definition and from which language the word came.

21. _____ _____

22. _____ _____

23. _____ _____

24. _____ _____

25. _____ _____

On Your Own: Well done! Keep on the lookout for new and unusual words that are being added to the English language all the time. Record them in your personal word dictionary.

Name: _____ Date: _____

Unit 6: Spelling/Usage: Oxymorons

Key Idea

- A pair of words that seem to contradict each other or just look silly together are called **oxymorons**.

  Examples: bittersweet   bitter = sad   sweet = happy

  bittersweet   =   pleasant sadness

  cold sweat   cold = not hot; sweat = what you do when it is hot

  cold sweat   =   sweat when it is not hot

Practice

Directions: Circle the oxymoron in each sentence. Then write a definition (or explanation) for the oxymoron on the line below the sentence.

1. The crowd was clearly confused by the directions to exit the stadium.

   _____

2. My friend ordered the jumbo shrimp for dinner at the fancy restaurant.

   _____

3. "What a fine mess you've gotten us in," said Ollie.

   _____

4. I almost always turn the lights off before I go to bed.

   _____

5. When we went to Aunt Mabel's for dinner, my mother told me to act naturally.

   _____

6. If it wasn't for bad luck, I wouldn't have any luck at all.

   _____

On Your Own: Write a sentence for each of these oxymorons: *sure bet, a little big.*

Name: _____ Date: _____

Unit 6: Spelling/Usage Test

Directions: Find the word that is spelled <u>incorrectly</u> in each pair. Fill in the circle for your choice.

1. ○ A. assistance
    ○ B. assistence

2. ○ A. obediance
    ○ B. obedience

3. ○ A. excellance
    ○ B. excellence

4. ○ A. patiance
    ○ B. patience

5. ○ A. differance
    ○ B. difference

6. ○ A. distance
    ○ B. distence

7. ○ A. possible
    ○ B. possable

8. ○ A. sensible
    ○ B. sensable

9. ○ A. impossible
    ○ B. impossable

10. ○ A. allowible
    ○ B. allowable

11. ○ A. permanence
    ○ B. permanance

12. ○ A. resistence
    ○ B. resistance

13. ○ A. annoyence
    ○ B. annoyance

14. ○ A. violence
    ○ B. violance

15. ○ A. absence
    ○ B. absance

16. ○ A. importence
    ○ B. importance

17. ○ A. eatible
    ○ B. eatable

18. ○ A. reliable
    ○ B. reliible

19. ○ A. lovible
    ○ B. lovable

20. ○ A. perishible
    ○ B. perishable

Name: _____ Date: _____

Unit 6: Spelling/Usage Test (cont.)

Directions: Write the word, spelling it correctly, for each definition below:

21. A person who studies the practice of pharmacy _____

22. The study of minerals _____

23. A physician practicing the branch of
     medicine dealing with the nervous system _____

24. The study of water _____

25. The study of the earth _____

26. A place where people walk on the side
     of a street _____

27. Sparkling gem named after the Rhine River in
     Germany _____

28. A toy bear named after Teddy Roosevelt _____

29. A flat, sweet cracker named after Sylvester
     Graham, a vegetarian _____

30. Ground where people are allowed to camp _____

Directions: Identify the oxymorons in the following sentences by circling them.

31. My father describes my uncle as a clever fool for investing all his money in the project.

32. Tiger Woods was guest host on "Golf Digest Tonight."

33. Delia's new purse is genuine imitation ostrich.

34. The flowers in the garden were awfully pretty.

35. Prisoners of war describe their captivity as a living death.

Name: _____ Date: _____

Unit 7: Function Words: Conjunctions

Key Ideas

- A **conjunction** is a grammatical connector that links sentence parts and expresses relationships between ideas.

- **Conjunctions** can signal cause and effect; show time sequences; or indicate alternatives, parallels, or contrasts.

  Example 1:　**Since** his boss was late, Glenn was reprimanded for being late. (cause and effect)

  Example 2:　**While** Alicia was an exchange student in Paris, she visited the Eiffel Tower. (time sequence)

  Example 3:　You can walk, **or** you can run to the park.　　(alternatives)

  Example 4:　**Either** Heather **or** Hannah will get the job.　　(parallels)

  Example 5:　Mrs. Taylor is thinner this year **than** last year. (contrast)

- Some common **conjunctions** are *and, but, or, for, nor, yet, so, although, that, than, because, before, during, whoever, after, unless, since, when, while,* and *wherever.*

Practice

Directions: Underline all conjunctions; identify what function the conjunction plays in the sentence.

1. Fabio ate seven slices of pizza and drank two pitchers of iced tea.

   _____

2. Mr. Tania still works for the button company that he started with thirty years ago.

   _____

3. While Ricardo was playing freshman football, he was also playing on the soccer team.

   _____

4. My Aunt Ethel wouldn't go to the mall because there would be too many people there.

   _____

5. Alexandra studied world religions intensely, so she should know about religious holidays.

   _____

6. First, we go to the booth to get the tickets.

   _____

7. Samantha is taller than he. _____

Name: _____ Date: _____

Unit 7: Function Words: Comparative Conjunctions

Key Ideas

- A special type of conjunction is a **comparative conjunction**. This conjunction has two parts—for example, *so ... that* and *as ... as.*

    Example 1:   Sam was **so** scared **that** he was shaking like a leaf.

    Example 2:   She is not **as** smart **as** she thinks she is.

- **Comparative conjunctions** usually introduce ideas that express "how much" or "to what extent."

    Example 1:   He is such a kind man **that** kids usually take advantage of him.

    Example 2:   This computer works more efficiently **than** the old one did.

Practice

Directions: Use a comparative conjunction and a dependent clause to revise the sentences below.

1. The day was hot. (How hot was it?)

    _____

2. We are distant relatives. (How distant are you?)

    _____

3. The movie was entertaining. The company was entertaining. (Which one was more entertaining?)

    _____

    _____

4. Kelly performed her skating routine well. (How well did she perform?)

    _____

    _____

5. The deck around the house was dangerous. (How dangerous was it?)

    _____

    _____

On Your Own: Write your own sentence, and then give it to a friend to add an interesting comparative conjunction.

Name: _____ Date: _____

Unit 7: Function Words: Coordinating Conjunctions

Key Ideas

- **Conjunctions** connect words or groups of words to each other and tell something about the relationship between these words. Some common conjunctions are: *and, but, or, for, nor, so, yet, although, because, when, while, wherever, since, unless,* and *whenever.*

- **Coordinating conjunctions** are conjunctions that connect things that are somewhat equal, like two sentences, two nouns, or two verbs.
  Example 1: Alicia watches television all day **and** pays for it afterwards.
  Example 2: She is all alone, **yet** she doesn't seem lonely.

- There are seven **coordinating conjunction**s: *and, but, or, for, nor, so,* and *yet.*

- When using the **coordinating conjunctions** *and, but, or, for, nor, so,* and *yet* to connect two sentences, put a comma before the conjunction.
  Example: I'm going to the mall, **but** you aren't coming with me.

Practice

Directions: Combine the sentences below using a coordinating conjunction and a comma as necessary.

1. I went to the mall over the weekend. I didn't buy anything.

   _____

   _____

2. Mollie called 911. Martha opened the door for the rescue squad.

   _____

   _____

3. Robin wanted to be rich. He wanted to be famous. He didn't care which.

   _____

   _____

4. Tawana told everyone about the broken fence. No one believed her.

   _____

   _____

5. Does anyone have lunch money? Should we borrow some?

   _____

   _____

Name: _____ Date: _____

Unit 7: Function Words: Coordinating Conjunctions (cont.)

6. Janet wanted to go out to lunch with her friends. She didn't have any money.

   _____

   _____

7. Marshall knew his brother wasn't coming. He sat in the station and waited anyway.

   _____

   _____

8. The teacher heard my story. She believed every word of it.

   _____

   _____

9. The robber was sentenced to ten years in jail. He was a very bad man.

   _____

   _____

10. LaVonn was not especially friendly. She wasn't popular either.

   _____

   _____

Directions: Make up a sentence using each of the coordinating conjunctions below. Be sure to punctuate correctly.

1. and _____

   _____

2. but _____

   _____

3. or _____

   _____

4. for _____

   _____

5. nor _____

   _____

On Your Own: Write a paragraph about what you usually do over the weekend. Try to use all seven coordinating conjunctions correctly in your paragraph.

Name: _____ Date: _____

Unit 7: Function Words: Prepositions

Key Ideas

- A **preposition** connects the word, phrase, or clause that follows it with some other element in the sentence.

  Example: Lakeisha had been in a discussion **with** her attorney.
  With connects the attorney with the discussion.

- A **preposition** can be a single word (*to, with*) or a phrase (*according to, as well as, because of, and contrary to*).

  Example 1:   Buddy walked **by** my house.
  Example 2:   John drove **contrary to** his parents' wishes.

- Some common **prepositions** are: *above, after, around, at, away, before, behind, by, from, in, into, of, on, over, through,* and *under.*

Practice

Directions: Circle the prepositions in each sentence and underline the two words or phrases that the preposition connects.

1. Whenever we go to the show, I like to get popcorn.

2. A large dolphin swam toward our boat.

3. The airplane flew into the night sky.

4. Smoke from our campfire filled the air.

5. The child leaned against her father while riding the snowmobile.

6. Her baby-fine hair blew in the wind.

7. After the race, the Smitson kids headed to the showers.

8. Little children were making angels in the snow.

9. Fatima jumped off the table into the snowbank.

10. Mother scrambled up the nearest hill after she spotted the bear.

Name: _____ Date: _____

Unit 7: Function Words: Prepositional Phrases

Key Ideas

- A **preposition** connects the word, phrase, or clause that follows it with some other element in the sentence.

    Example: Cameren went **to** the <u>mall</u> **for** new <u>shoes</u>.

- A **prepositional phrase** is a group of words that begins with a **preposition** and ends with a noun or pronoun—the "object" of the preposition.

    Example: East St. Louis is <u>near the Mississippi River</u>.

    Near is the preposition, and *Mississippi River* is the object of the preposition. *Near the Mississippi River* is the prepositional phrase.

Practice

Directions: Underline the prepositional phrase in each sentence. Circle the objects of the prepositions.

1. The skater on ice had grace and agility.

2. My dog drinks water from the bathroom toilet.

3. Our soccer team played against Rochester in the semifinals.

4. My mother and I agreed to meet at five o'clock near the food court.

5. Clark Kent disappeared into the phone booth and reappeared as Superman.

6. Several children sitting beside the alarm speaker were startled when it blared.

7. Trixie found her socks under the bed.

8. Beneath the snow I found my sled; it was lying on the deck.

9. Ms. Altman had fallen behind in her work.

10. We visited Walt Disney World during our vacation.

On Your Own: Arrange the members of your family for a family photograph. Use the following prepositions, and write a paragraph describing how everyone is to be arranged.

beside   **near**   **at**   **from**   **behind**

Name: _____ Date: _____

Unit 7: Function Words: Determiners 1

Key Ideas

- A **determiner** is a word like *a, the, our, this,* or *Sharon's* that signals that a noun will follow, if not immediately, then shortly.

    Example: Where did you hide **the** peanut butter *cookies*?
    The is the determiner; *cookies* is the noun.

- Some words are always **determiners**.
- Articles like *a, an,* and *the* are always determiners.

    Example 1:   **A** new *car* is always fun to take to **the** *beach.*
    Example 2:   Dad says that Mom made **an** honest *man* of him.

- Some possessive pronouns like *my, her, its, your, their,* and *whose* are **determiners**.

    Example: **Whose** green *coat* was left on **your** *bed*?

- The indefinite pronoun *every* is always a **determiner**.

    Example: Dad says "no" **every** *time* I ask if I can go to the dance.

Practice

Directions: Identify the determiners in the following sentences by circling them, and then underline the noun that the determiner signals.

1. Where did you hide the Christmas presents?

2. A new puppy usually brings excitement to the house.

3. I didn't like your answer to their question.

4. Mr. Minn gave a dollar to every person in the room.

5. The skater put her skates and towels in her bag before she left the arena.

6. The Komodo dragon sank its teeth into the man's leg.

7. Every second of every day, your long-distance plan is in effect.

8. The street was so hot, it burned a hole through my shoes.

On Your Own: Look at the first paragraph of the next story you have to read in literature. Count the number of determiners in the paragraph. Compare with classmates to see if they agree with your count.

Name: _____ Date: _____

Unit 7: Function Words: Determiners 2

Key Ideas

- **Determiners** signal that a noun will follow, if not immediately, then shortly.
    Example: Where did you hide **the** peanut butter *cookies*?

- Some words are always **determiners**: *a, the, my, their, whose, every.*
    Example 1:   **A** new *car* is always fun to take to **the** *beach.*
    Example 2:   **Her** apple *pie* is much better than mine.
    Example 3:   She got **every** *item* on sale.

- **Some nouns and pronouns** frequently function as **determiners** (when they signal that a noun or pronoun will follow).

- **Possessives** (like *his, everyone's, Cecilia's*) sometimes function as **determiners**.
    Example: Giving the speech was **his** *responsibility.*

- **Demonstrative pronouns** (*this, that, these, those*) sometimes function as **determiners**.
    Example: You must pack **these** *pajamas* for the trip.

- **Indefinite pronouns** (*each, either, neither, all, some, many, much, any, few, more, less,* and so on) can sometimes function as **determiners**.
    Example: **Few** *actors* actually achieve fame and fortune.

- **Interrogative pronouns** (*which, what*) can sometimes function as **determiners**.
    Example: The doctors could not tell **which** *virus* she contracted.

- **Cardinal numbers** (*one, two, three,* and so on) can sometimes function as **determiners**.
    Example: The police showed us pictures of **four** *muggers.*

Practice

Directions: Identify the determiners in the following sentences by circling them, and then underline the noun that the determiner signals.

1. My teacher sent our story to *Reader's Digest.*

2. The cold weather has ruined the fruit crops in two states.

3. Every year the monsoon season causes flooding in that section of the country.

4. Which kind of soda will most kids buy this year?

5. The three projects we were assigned were hard for many students.

6. Which one of these do you like?

7. Each student is responsible for his own project.

Name: _____ Date: _____

Unit 7: Function Words Test

Directions: Identify the part of speech underlined in each sentence by darkening the correct circle.

1. You might as well leave, <u>since</u> you are so late arriving.
   - ○ A. coordinating conjunction
   - ○ B. comparative conjunction
   - ○ C. preposition
   - ○ D. prepositional phrase
   - ○ E. determiner

2. <u>Martha's</u> bracelet was made of real diamonds.
   - ○ A. coordinating conjunction
   - ○ B. comparative conjunction
   - ○ C. preposition
   - ○ D. prepositional phrase
   - ○ E. determiner

3. The trip will <u>either</u> be a complete disaster <u>or</u> a lot of fun.
   - ○ A. coordinating conjunction
   - ○ B. comparative conjunction
   - ○ C. preposition
   - ○ D. prepositional phrase
   - ○ E. determiner

4. <u>Her</u> pajamas had clouds and suns all over them.
   - ○ A. coordinating conjunction
   - ○ B. comparative conjunction
   - ○ C. preposition
   - ○ D. prepositional phrase
   - ○ E. determiner

5. The man he was following disappeared <u>into the alley</u> that bisected the street.
   - ○ A. coordinating conjunction
   - ○ B. comparative conjunction
   - ○ C. preposition
   - ○ D. prepositional phrase
   - ○ E. determiner

6. He argued his case <u>before</u> the Supreme Court.
   - ○ A. coordinating conjunction
   - ○ B. comparative conjunction
   - ○ C. preposition
   - ○ D. prepositional phrase
   - ○ E. determiner

7. I'm going to the Philippines, <u>but</u> my family isn't coming with me.
   - ○ A. coordinating conjunction
   - ○ B. comparative conjunction
   - ○ C. preposition
   - ○ D. prepositional phrase
   - ○ E. determiner

8. Mrs. Pinkney was <u>such</u> a mean old lady <u>that</u> the neighborhood kids were all afraid of her.
   - ○ A. coordinating conjunction
   - ○ B. comparative conjunction
   - ○ C. preposition
   - ○ D. prepositional phrase
   - ○ E. determiner

9. Joey keeps driving <u>by my house</u> looking longingly at my swimming pool.
   - ○ A. coordinating conjunction
   - ○ B. comparative conjunction
   - ○ C. preposition
   - ○ D. prepositional phrase
   - ○ E. determiner

10. <u>After the movie</u>, my boyfriend and I walked to the restaurant for a snack.
    - ○ A. coordinating conjunction
    - ○ B. comparative conjunction
    - ○ C. preposition
    - ○ D. prepositional phrase
    - ○ E. determiner

Name: _____ Date: _____

Topic: _____

Type of Writing: _____

Teacher Scoring Rubric for Evaluating Student Writing

Directions: Circle the number that best describes the quality of the writing.

1 **Not Yet:**   A bare beginning; writer not yet showing any control
2 **Emerging:**   Need for revision outweighs strengths; isolated moments hint at what the writer has in mind
3 **Developing:** Strengths and need for revision are about equal; about halfway home
4 **Effective:**   On balance, the strengths outweigh the weaknesses; a small amount of revision is needed
5 **Strong:**   Shows control and skill in this trait; many strengths present
6 **Wow!**   Exceeds expectations

Features	Not Yet	Emerging	Developing	Effective	Strong
Ideas: The paper is clear and focused; it holds the reader's attention; relevant anecdotes and details enrich the central theme.	1	2	3	4	5
Organization: The organization enhances and showcases the central idea or theme. The order and structure of information is compelling and moves the reader through the text.	1	2	3	4	5
Voice: The writer speaks directly to the reader in a way that is individual, compelling, and engaging. The writer crafts the writing with an awareness and respect for the audience and the purpose for writing.	1	2	3	4	5
Word Choice: Words convey the intended message in a precise, interesting, and natural way. The words are powerful and engaging.	1	2	3	4	5
Sentence Fluency: The writing has an easy flow, rhythm, and cadence. Sentences are well built, with strong and varied structure that invites expressive oral reading.	1	2	3	4	5
Conventions: The writer demonstrates a good and age-appropriate grasp of standard writing conventions—spelling, punctuation, capitalization, grammar, usage, and paragraphing.	1	2	3	4	5
Presentation: The form and presentation of the text enhance the reader's ability to understand and connect with the message. The piece is pleasing to the eye.	1	2	3	4	5

Comments: _____

_____

Name: _____ **Date:** _____

Topic: _____

Type of Writing: _____

Student Scoring Rubric for Evaluating Peer Writing

Directions: Circle the number that best describes the quality of the writing.

1 **Not Yet:**   A bare beginning; writer not yet showing any control
2 **Emerging:**   Need for revision outweighs strengths; isolated moments hint at what the writer has in mind
3 **Developing:** Strengths and need for revision are about equal; about halfway home
4 **Effective:**   On balance, the strengths outweigh the weaknesses; a small amount of revision is needed
5 **Strong:**   Shows control and skill in this trait; many strengths present
6 **Wow!**   Exceeds expectations

Features	Not Yet	Emerging	Developing	Effective	Strong
Ideas: Is the paper clear and focused? Does it hold the reader's attention?	1	2	3	4	5
Organization: Does the organization enhance the central idea and move the reader through the text?	1	2	3	4	5
Voice: Does the writer speak directly to the reader in a way that is individual, compelling, and engaging?	1	2	3	4	5
Word Choice: Do the words convey the intended message in a precise, interesting, and natural way? Are the words powerful and engaging?	1	2	3	4	5
Sentence Fluency: Does the writing have an easy flow, rhythm, and cadence? Are sentences well built, with strong and varied structure that invites expressive oral reading?	1	2	3	4	5
Conventions: Does the writer demonstrate a good grasp of spelling, punctuation, capitalization, grammar, usage, and paragraphing?	1	2	3	4	5
Presentation: Does the form and presentation of the paper enhance the reader's ability to understand and connect with the message? Is the piece pleasing to the eye?	1	2	3	4	5

Comments: _____

Name: _____   Date: _____

Section III: Student Rubric for Evaluating Writing

Topic: _____

Type of Writing: *Expository*   *Persuasive*   *Narrative*

Directions: Check those statements that apply to your piece of writing.

_____   I have a clear and interesting topic that I care about.

_____   My writing is based on my own experience or my own investigation of the topic.

_____   I can sum up my main point in one sentence: _____

            _____

_____   I have a strong beginning that "grabs" my reader's attention.

_____   I have included all important events in the order of their happening.

_____   My writing is easy to follow; each point leads to the next point.

_____   I *show* things happening rather than *telling* about them.

_____   My writing has energy, enthusiasm, and confidence and sounds like me.

_____   My language is appropriate to my topic and audience.

_____   My story reads well out loud.

_____   My writing reaches out to "grab" my reader's attention and holds it right up to the end.

_____   I have a strong ending that leaves my reader satisfied.

_____   There are no significant errors in my paper.

_____   I revised and edited this paper carefully.

Comments: _____

_____

_____

_____

Answer Keys

Unit 1: Writing Skills Test (p. 14–16)
1. A	2. C	3. B	4. D
5. B	6. A	7. B	8. D
9. C	10. C	11. A	12. D
13. D	14. C	15. B	

16.–20. Teacher check using Ideas criteria.

Unit 2: Writing Skills Test (p. 30–32)
1. A	2. D	3. C	4. C
5. B	6. C	7. A	8. D
9. B	10. A	11. D	12. C
13. B	14. C	15. A	

16.–20. Teacher check using Organization criteria.

Unit 3: Writing Skills Test (p. 45–49)
1. B	2. C	3. D	4. C
5. D	6. D	7. A	8. D
9. C	10. B	11. A	12. A, D
13. B	14. C	15. A, B, C, D	

16.–20. Teacher check using Voice criteria.

Unit 4: Figurative Language (p. 55)
1. She, daisy; simile
2. bed, rock; simile
3. heart, rainbow; metaphor
4. gulley, Grand Canyon; simile
5. flashlight, beacon; metaphor

Unit 4: Fluency (p. 70)
1. a	2. a	3. a	4. b	5. b

Unit 4: Fluency Problems 1 (p. 71)
Teacher check correct sentences.
1. not, nobody   2. Don't, none
3. not, nothing   4. not, no
5. not, none

Unit 4: Fluency Problems 2 (p. 72)
1. No variation in length or complexity
2. Wordy
3. No variation in length or complexity
4. No variation in beginnings
5. No problems

Unit 4: Writing Skills Test (p. 75–78)
1. A	2. D	3. A	4. C
5. D	6. A	7. C	8. D
9. B	10. A	11. C	12. C
13. B	14. D	15. B	16. B
17. C	18. A	19. B	

20.–25. Teacher check using Word Choice and Fluency criteria.

Section II: Conventions of Writing (p. 84)

No More circus!

For my birthday, mom and dad said I could redecorate my bedroom. The last time it was decroated was when I was for years old. Its time to say good-bye to the circis theme—no more big top canapy, elephants, lions, tiggers, or clowns. My new wallpaper and bedspread will have Race cars Monster trucks and Motorcycles on them. My parents are even going to by me a computer desk and a computer, so I can do my homework in my room ill have the coolest bedroom ever!

Unit 5: Punctuation: Commas 1 (p. 85)
1. He has plundered our seas, ravaged our coasts, burnt our towns, and destroyed the lives of our people.   —Declaration of Independence
2. The long, twisting, muddy road led to the private cabin in the woods.
3. To win a gold medal, Bonnie needed a lot of luck.
4. When I opened the junk drawer, the scissors, tape, ruler, and stapler fell out.
5. At the video arcade, Jason lost all of his allowance, his jacket, and his package.
6. To make hot chocolate, heat the milk slowly, stirring constantly, and then add the mix.
7. For dinner, we had a choice of steak, chicken, or seafood.
8. When in doubt, ask someone for advice.

Unit 5: Punctuation: Commas 2 (p. 86)
Last week, I saw my friend, Randy, in the bookstore. She was sitting in a chair with three books, two magazines, and four pens. "Yo," I said. When she saw me, she winked, smiled, and said, "Hi!" I asked her if she was waiting for her mother, Helen, to come pick her up. Nodding her head, she said that she had been waiting here, at the photo mart, and at the doctor's for her mom to finish her shopping, her yoga lesson, and her errands. "Once she finishes," she said, "I'll get to go home!"

Unit 5: Punctuation: Dashes (p. 87)
1. Katie knows how to cook three things—spaghetti, egg sandwiches, and macaroni and cheese.
2. Robbie—my all-time favorite friend—was absent today.
3. Are you sure you have the right phone number—555-2718?

4. The person I least wanted to see showed up at the dance—Grant Fowler.
5. Bob Marley—a really annoying person—sits behind me in social studies.

Unit 5: Punctuation: Parentheses (p. 88)
1. Our topics today are (a) election of officers, (b) forming committees, and (c) setting the date for the next dance.
2. David Hamilton (you met him last Sunday) will be at the wedding reception.
3. Do you know where the Society for the Prevention of Cruelty to Animals (SPCA) is located?
4. This map (I am sure it is accurate) should lead us to the treasure.
5. Marysia (she is my cousin from Croatia) is coming for a visit this summer.
6. You can call our family 800 number (1-800-555-6566) to reach me anytime.
7. Turn to Chapter 3 in your book (pages 73–91).
8. In social studies, we read about the Klu Klux Klan's (KKK) activity during the pre-civil rights era.

Unit 5: Punctuation: End Punctuation (p. 89)
1. ! or .   2. ?   3. .
4. ! or .   5. ?   6. .
7. ! or .   8. ?   9. .
10. !

Unit 5: Punctuation: Semicolons 1 (p. 90)
1. b   2. a   3. b
4. a   5. a   6. b

Unit 5: Punctuation: Semicolons 2 (p. 91)
1. b   2. a   3. b   4. b
5. b   6. b   7. a   8. b

Unit 5: Punctuation: Semicolons 3 (p. 92)
1. a   2. a   3. b
4. a   5. a   6. a

Unit 5: Punctuation: Apostrophes 1 (p. 93–94)
1. queen's   2. hero's
3. its   4. ladies'
5. yours   6. bride's
7. horses'   8. mine
9. Phil's   10. parents'

1. Malcolm's dog is wagging its tail.
2. Zane's sister is the star player on the girls' basketball team.
3. I do not always agree with my teacher's interpretations of the stories we read.

4. Sarah's mother called the school and said that she was sick today.
5. Your hamster's food is in its dish on the teacher's desk.

Unit 5: Punctuation: Apostrophes 2 (p. 95)
1. Isn't it a beautiful day?
2. They're on the teacher's desk behind her calendar.
3. Nicholas's shoes are always in the middle of the floor.
4. Aren't the children's stories this year better than last year's stories?
5. We're studying South America's geography and Brazil's language, Portuguese.
6. It doesn't look like rain for today's baseball game.
7. I just can't do what the coach wants me to do with the team's equipment.
8. Ira's car is in my father's shop waiting for its tune-up.

Unit 5: Punctuation Test (p. 96–99)
1. C   2. B
3. A   4. B or D
5. C   6. A
7. A   8. C
9. D   10. C
11. C   12. A
13. B or D   14. C
15. B   16. A or B
17. A or B   18. C
19. A or B   20. A
21. C   22. B
23. B   24. C
25. D   26. B
27. B   28. B
29. B   30. B

Unit 6: Spelling/Usage: Suffixes (p. 100)
1. assistance   2. abundance
3. excellence   4. patience
5. obedience   6. distance
7. difference   8. repentance
9. avoidance   10. succulence
11. permanence   12. convenience
13. elegance   14. resistance
15. importance   16. absence
17. imminence   18. annoyance
19. violence   20. defiance

Unit 6: Spelling/Usage: Suffixes (p. 101)
1. eligible   2. perishable
3. lovable   4. impossible
5. reliable   6. sensible
7. eatable   8. possible
9. edible   10. readable

11. enjoyable
12. expressible
13. acceptable
14. playable
15. washable
16. payable
17. incredible
18. conquerable
19. legible
20. plausible

Unit 6: Spelling/Usage: Suffixes (p. 102)
1. one who studies the cosmos
2. the study of music
3. the study of animals
4. one who studies the earth
5. the study of water
6. one who studies volcanoes
7. the study of radiant energy
8. one who studies fossils
9. the study of pharmacy (drugs, medicine)
10. one who studies the psyche (the mind)

Unit 6: Spelling/Usage: Compound Words (p. 103)
1. doorknob; knob on a door
2. lightweight; light in weight
3. long-legged; long in the legs
4. wiretapping; to tap a wire (listen in on a phone line)
5. manhunt; a hunt for a man
6. newsstand; a stand for newspapers, etc.

Unit 6: Spelling/Usage: Borrowed Words (p. 104–105)
1. mosquito: a two-winged insect; Spanish/Portuguese
2. guitar: a stringed musical instrument; French/Spanish/Greek
3. karate: a way of fighting without using weapons; Japanese
4. jungle: wild, overgrown land; Hindi
5. pajamas: nightclothes; Sanskrit/Hindi
6. shampoo: to wash with soap; Hindi
7. souvenir: a memento of a visit or trip; French
8. casserole: a dish in which food is both cooked and served; French
9. tomato: a South American plant with red fruit; Spanish
10. chocolate: a beverage made with roasted and ground cacao seeds, milk or water, and sugar; Spanish
11. rodeo: a cattle roundup; Spanish
12. patio: an outdoor space for dining; Spanish
13. camouflage: concealment by wearing clothing with protective coloring; French
14. ketchup: a condiment; Malay
15. chipmunk: a striped, terrestrial squirrel; Ojibwa
16. bagel: a glazed roll of baked dough; Yiddish
17. vanilla: a seed pod of climbing, tropical orchids; Spanish
18. tulip: a bulbous plant in the lily family; Turkish
19. zebra: a swift African horse; Italian
20. knapsack: a sturdy bag with straps; German
21.–25. Answers will vary

Unit 6: Spelling/Usage: Oxymorons (p. 106)
1. Clearly confused: *clearly* contradicts *confused*
2. Jumbo shrimp: large/small
3. Fine mess: A mess is not fine.
4. Almost always: *Always* does not mean some of the time.
5. Act naturally: If you want to be natural, don't act.
6. Bad luck: Luck is considered a positive thing, not a negative.

Unit 6: Spelling/Usage Test (p. 107–108)
1. B
2. A
3. A
4. A
5. A
6. B
7. B
8. B
9. B
10. A
11. B
12. A
13. A
14. B
15. B
16. A
17. A
18. B
19. A
20. A
21. pharmacist
22. mineralogy
23. neurologist
24. hydrology
25. geology
26. sidewalk
27. rhinestone
28. Teddy bear
29. graham cracker
30. campground
31. clever fool
32. guest host
33. genuine imitation
34. awfully pretty
35. living death

Unit 7: Function Words: Conjunctions (p. 109)
1. and; connection
2. that; cause and effect
3. While; time sequence
4. because; cause and effect
5. so; cause and effect
6. First; time sequence
7. than; contrast

Unit 7: Function Words: Comparative Conjunctions (p. 110)
Answers will vary.

Unit 7: Function Words: Coordinating Conjunctions (p. 111–112)
Answers will vary.

Unit 7: Function Words: Prepositions (p. 113)

1. Whenever we go (to) the show, I like to get popcorn.
2. A large dolphin swam (toward) our boat.
3. The airplane flew (into) the night sky.
4. Smoke (from) our campfire filled the air.
5. The child leaned (against) her father while riding the snowmobile.
6. Her baby-fine hair blew (in) the wind.
7. (After) the race, the Smitson kids headed (to) the showers.
8. Little children were making angels (in) the snow.
9. Fatima jumped (off) the table (into) the snowbank.
10. Mother scrambled (up) the nearest hill after she spotted the bear.

Unit 7: Function Words: Prepositional Phrases (p. 114)

1. The skater on (ice) had grace and agility.
2. My dog drinks water from the bathroom (toilet).
3. Our soccer team played against (Rochester) in the (semifinals).
4. My mother and I agreed to meet at (five o'clock) near the food (court).
5. Clark Kent disappeared into the phone (booth) and came out as Superman.
6. Several children beside the alarm (speaker) were startled when it blared.
7. Trixie found her socks under the (bed).
8. Beneath the (snow) I found my sled; it was lying on the (deck).
9. Ms. Altman had fallen behind in her (work).
10. We visited Walt Disney World during our (vacation).

Unit 7: Function Words: Determiners 1 (p. 115)

1. Where did you hide (the) Christmas presents?
2. (A) new puppy usually brings excitement to (the) house.
3. I didn't like (your) answer to (their) question.
4. Mr. Minn gave (a) dollar to (every) person in (the) room.
5. (The) skater put (her) skates and towels in (her) bag before she left (the) arena.
6. (The) Komodo dragon sank (its) teeth (into) the man's leg.
7. (Every) second of (every) day (your) long-distance plan is in effect.
8. (The) street was so hot, it burned (a) hole through (my) shoes.

Unit 7: Function Words: Determiners 2 (p. 116)

1. (My) teacher sent (our) story to *Reader's Digest*.
2. (The) cold weather has ruined (the) fruit crops in (two) states.
3. (Every) year (the) monsoon season causes flooding in (that) section of (the) country.
4. (Which) kind of soda will (most) kids buy (this) year?
5. (The) (three) projects we were assigned were hard for (many) students.
6. (Which) one of these do you like?
7. (Each) student is responsible for (his) own project.

Unit 7: Function Words Test (p. 117)

1. A	2. E
3. B	4. E
5. D	6. C
7. A	8. B
9. D	10. D